Management Control Systems in Japan

As the world's third-ranking economic power, Japan's style of management, such as the lifetime employment system, the seniority system, and an enterprise union, has been well studied. However, little else is known about the Japanese management control systems (MCSs) and management accounting systems, which are significantly different from other economic powers.

This book sheds light on Japanese MCSs and the differences with those of the United States, illustrated with examples from Mitsubishi Electric, Kao, and more. This book aids not only researchers in management accounting, but also provides more useful insight for international investors and management accountants that can prove useful in business management.

Takashi Shimizu is Professor at the Graduate School of Accountancy, Waseda University, and President of the Tokyo Chapter of Institute of Management Accountants. He was a member of the Japan Certified Public Accountant Examination Committee from 2006 to 2008.

Routledge Frontiers of Business Management

For a full list of titles in this series, please visit www.routledge.com/series/rfbm

1 **Managing Innovation and Cultural Management in the Digital Era**
The case of the National Palace Museum
Edited by Rua-Huan Tsaih and Tzu-Shian Han

2 **Managing Convergence in Innovation**
The new paradigm of technological innovation
Edited by Kong-rae Lee

3 **Corporate Sustainability Assessments**
Sustainability practices of multinational enterprises in Thailand
Edited by Jerome D. Donovan, Cheree Topple, Eryadi K. Masli and Teerin Vanichseni

4 **Knowledge Spillover-based Strategic Entrepreneurship**
Edited by João J. Ferreira, Leo-Paul Dana and Vanessa Ratten

5 **Japanese Management**
International perspectives
Hitoshi Iwashita

6 **Strategic Human Resource Management in China**
A Multiple Perspective
Min Min, Mary Bambacas and Ying Zhu

7 **Fostering Local Entrepreneurship in a Multinational Enterprise**
Joe J. Amberg and Sara L. McGaughey

8 **Digital Business and Sustainable Development**
Asian Perspectives
Yongrok Choi

9 **Management Control Systems in Japan**
Takashi Shimizu

Management Control Systems in Japan

Takashi Shimizu

Routledge
Taylor & Francis Group
LONDON AND NEW YORK

First published 2017 by Routledge

2 Park Square, Milton Park, Abingdon, Oxfordshire OX14 4RN
52 Vanderbilt Avenue, New York, NY 10017

Routledge is an imprint of the Taylor & Francis Group, an informa business

First issued in paperback 2019

British Library Cataloguing-in-Publication Data
A catalogue record for this book is available from the British Library

Library of Congress Cataloging-in-Publication Data
A catalog record for this book has been requested

ISBN: 978-1-138-12275-8 (hbk)
ISBN: 978-0-367-35052-9 (pbk)

Typeset in Galliard
by Apex CoVantage, LLC

Contents

List of figures vii
List of tables viii
Acknowledgments x

1 Introduction: what are management control systems in Japanese companies? 1

2 Management control systems: definitions and development 11

3 Cost allocation systems: ABC versus Japanese cost accounting innovation 20

4 A challenge to better budgeting in Japanese companies 35

5 Management in decentralized Japanese companies 54

6 Balanced Scorecard versus the Japanese system 68

7 Performance measures: ROI, ROS, ROE, and EVA® 80

8 Management of advertising expenses in KAO 92

9 Transfer pricing in Mitsubishi Electric 106

10 Beyond budgeting or new budgeting? The case of Disco 119

11 Microprofit centers: amoeba system in Kyocera 134

12 The story of a comeback from bankruptcy: Japan Airlines 149

Index 161

Figures

2.1	Strategic implementing system	15
2.2	Management control systems package	17
3.1	Allocation system of overhead costs by using the direct method	21
3.2	Cost flow in ABC systems	22
3.3	The process of ABC systems	23
3.4	Cost structure	26
3.5	Grouping step-down method (1)	28
3.6	Grouping step-down method (2)	30
5.1	A functional system	58
5.2	A division system	59
6.1	The components of Balanced Scorecard	69
6.2	The strategy map of a chain restaurant company	72
6.3	The structure of the scorecard	73
6.4	The flow of Hoshin-Kanri	77
7.1	Business structure	81
8.1	Flow of ABB	95
8.2	The Kao way	99
8.3	Strategic implementing system in Kao	103
9.1	The matrix income statement	116
9.2	Strategic implementing system in ME	117
10.1	Rolling forecast	123
10.2	Forecast system in NEC	124
10.3	Increasing corporate value	127
10.4	Strategic implementing system in Disco	131
11.1	Sales amoeba and production amoeba	138
11.2	Rolling forecast in Kyocera	142
11.3	Feedforward and feedback management in Kyocera	142
11.4	Open book management in Kyocera	143
11.5	Strategic implementing system in Kyocera	146
12.1	JAL organization chart in April 2016	156
12.2	Strategic implementing system in JAL	159

Tables

3.1 The current ratio of overhead costs to manufacturing costs 25
3.2 Allocation methods 27
3.3 Dual-rate method or single-rate method? 32
3.4 Allocation bases of operating department costs 33
4.1 The type of industry of the respondents 36
4.2 Do companies use budgetary management or not? 37
4.3 Problems with budgeting systems 38
4.4 Are you satisfied with your budgeting system? 39
4.5 Time for budget preparation 39
4.6 Predictability 40
4.7 Frequency of a revenue forecast 42
4.8 Reliability of a revenue forecast 43
4.9 Revising revenue targets downward or not? 44
4.10 Revising cost targets downward or not? 44
4.11 Revising revenue targets upward or not? 45
4.12 Revising cost targets upward or not? 46
4.13 Target setting in divisions 46
4.14 Attempt to make targets in divisions stretch 47
4.15 Performance measurement items of profit centers 48
4.16 Performance measurement items of profit-center managers 49
4.17 Impact of the degree of budget attainment of managers on their bonuses 51
5.1 An income statement of a division (A) 61
5.2 An income statement of a division (B) 64
7.1 Financial measures that Japanese companies prefer 85
7.2 The status of the utilization of EVA® in major Japanese companies 85
7.3 ROE, ROS, and CT in the United Kingdom, the United States, and Japan 88
8.1 The products in Kao 97
8.2 Financial performance 97
8.3 Kao, P&G, and Unilever 98

8.4 Domain, product group, and main brands in the beauty care business 101
8.5 Income statement by brand 101
9.1 Manufacturing costs of products X and Y 108
9.2 Income statements (produced by using market-based transfer prices) 108
9.3 Income statements (produced by using cost basis transfer prices) 109
9.4 Income statements (produced by using cost plus profit basis) 110
9.5 Income statements: market-based prices vs. cost basis prices 111
9.6 Income statements (dual pricing) 112
9.7 List of groups in ME 113
9.8 Financial performance 114
9.9 ME, Hitachi, and Toshiba 114
9.10 Corporate mission and seven guiding principles 115
10.1 Beyond budgeting concept 120
10.2 Financial performance of Disco 126
11.1 Financial performance of Kyocera 136
11.2 The 12 management principles in Kyocera 137
11.3 Income statement and hourly efficiency in production amoebas 140
11.4 Forecasted income statement of production amoebas 141
11.5 Comparing the Kyocera system with the beyond budgeting model (1) 144
11.6 Comparing the Kyocera system with the beyond budgeting model (2) 145
12.1 Financial performance 151

Acknowledgments

I have learned (and still now learn) a lot of theories from many books and papers written by Americans, Europeans, and Asians, including Japanese authors. However, management accounting practices in Japanese companies sometimes stay one step ahead of these theories. Many managers from various companies in Japan are my mentors, who show real-world examples of management control systems.

I thank the following individuals for sharing with me their invaluable experiences. First, I would like to express my thanks to Naoto Matsuoka, the director of Mitsubishi Electric Information Systems Corporation. He has many business experiences in the management accounting world and always raises good questions about theories. He invited me to the Strategic Accounting Meeting at the Business Research Institute as a coordinator. Many ideas in this book are attributed to discussions at this meeting. Yoshinori Fujita from Kao at that time was a member of this meeting and showed me Kao's management system.

Yoshio Kobayashi from Disco Corporation and Yasushi Omori from Japan Airlines told me the marvelous stories of their companies. Naoki Hori from Kyocera Communication Systems gave me many insightful views of amoeba systems. Again, I would like to extend my thanks to all of them and other businesspersons with whom I met to discuss their practices.

Many other persons contributed to this book. Ryohei Yanagi is CFO of Eisai and an executive director of the Tokyo Chapter of Institute of Management Accountants. His management accounting ideas always inspire me. Ryouta Machida and Tomoyuki Onishi are doctoral students of the Graduate School of Commerce of Waseda University, and they helped me a lot.

Finally, my thanks go to the members of team Shimizu, who helped polish my drafts into pristine English. Daniel Dolan, a professor of the Graduate School of Accountancy of Waseda University is my colleague and also one of my best friends. I could not have finished writing this book without his proofreading and sound advice. Fujiko Shimizu is my wife and a translator. She read my rough drafts and checked their grammar in a careful manner. She is not only a translator but also a highly capable editor. Thank you for your support!

1 Introduction

What are management control systems in Japanese companies?

Key learning points

- Management control systems are critical to implementing business strategy.
- What are management control systems in Japan?
- How different are management control systems in Japan from those in the Western world?

1. What are management control systems?

The purpose of this book is to clarify the features of management control systems (MCSs) in Japanese companies by comparing them with MCSs that have developed mainly in the United States.

Why should the features of Japanese MCSs be clarified? The reason is that there are some important differences between Japanese and U.S. MCSs, and I want readers to know and understand Japanese MCSs. For example, in U.S. companies, it is believed that Balanced Scorecard (BSC) is an excellent management tool and all companies should use it. In contrast, not many Japanese companies use BSC, even though top management and managers in Japanese companies are cognizant of the advantages of using BSC. According to U.S. textbooks, this is considered to be poor strategy because BSC is widely known as the brightest management control system in the world.

I have studied textbooks and papers written about control functions and published mainly in the United States for years. Some of the ideas in these textbooks and papers are different from those proposed in Japanese books and papers and from what I have heard directly from managers of Japanese companies. As a native of Japan, I have in-depth knowledge about how MCSs are used by Japanese companies. However, when I explain Japanese MCSs to people from other countries, most of them ask me questions such as: Why do Japanese companies adopt a different system of MCSs from that explained in U.S. textbooks? Do those MCSs work effectively? If so, why? In this book, I answer those questions.

Before dealing with those questions, I first have to define MCSs. The next chapter describes the definition and development of MCSs in detail, but in the remainder of the present chapter, I would like to show the features of MCSs instinctively.

MCSs move people to right action

Kaplan and Norton (2000) described business activities in the theory of Balanced Scorecard as follows. Companies have a long-term goal to achieve. They set a goal as an idealized vision and always pursue it. This goal is often called a mission. Companies set mid-term objectives aligned with the mission and formulate a strategy as a route to achieve the objectives. The strategy takes a specific form on a strategy map and is disclosed to all employees. They understand the strategy and think about what to do through the strategy map. This point is important. A lot of authors, including Kaplan and Norton, say that what is most important in today's management is that companies align employees' efforts with objectives and make effective use of employees' talents and skills in order to carry out a strategy.

It is employees that lead a company. Therefore, to implement a strategy successfully, companies need to formulate an effective strategy, make it understandable to employees, and communicate the strategy to them repeatedly so that they can have a thorough grasp of it. Also, companies have to make certain that employees consider how to play a part in implementing the strategy, and then put their ideas into appropriate action.

As mentioned in detail in Chapter 2, Anthony et al. (1965) named these systems *management control systems.* In the latest book by Anthony and Govindarajan, the authors state that "management control is the process by which managers influence other members of the organization to implement the organization's strategies" (Anthony and Govindarajan, 2010, p. 6). As demonstrated by this definition, MCSs are aggregates of some systems that influence people. Each system needs to be linked so that the achievement of managers' objectives may directly lead to the achievement of an organization's goal. It is often said that suboptimal management decision making may result from a lack of alignment of managers' objectives with an organization's goals and from managers setting objectives that are too high and hard to reach.

Although the proper setting of an objective is a difficult issue, what is most important in setting an objective is how stretch objectives managers can set by themselves. If managers always do their best, companies can produce the best performance in any circumstances. Among Japanese companies, Toyota is a good example to exhibit this. All employees in Toyota always make every effort to produce higher performance through their own initiative, even though they are not forced to work hard by their boss. The more of these types of employees in a company, the higher its performance is.

2. What are management control systems in Japan?

My research field is management accounting, and I have been studying management control systems and strategic management systems (SMSs) for years. Because many theories about MCSs and SMSs, as well as performance management models such as *beyond budgeting*, were developed in the United States and Europe, I have translated some of these works into Japanese to introduce them to Japanese scholars, businesspersons, and students. Some examples include *Strategic Focused Organizations* (Kaplan and Norton, 2001), *Business Performance Measurement* (Neely, 2002), *Strategy Maps* (Kaplan and Norton, 2004), *Beyond Budgeting* (Hope and Fraser, 2005), *Balanced Scorecard: Step by Step, 2nd edition* (Niven, 2006), *Implementing Beyond Budgeting* (Bogsnes, 2009), and the like. These books are extremely insightful, but I doubt whether they can be perfectly applied to Japanese companies. For example, Kaplan and Norton (2000) advocated that one of three value propositions – operational excellence, product leadership, and customer intimacy – be selected by companies as an area of focus, and that companies should not pursue more than one value proposition, because pursuing multiple value propositions may result in all propositions being incomplete. Is this really true?

Japanese companies always pursue operational excellence, product leadership, and customer intimacy simultaneously. That is, the goal of Japanese companies is to offer customers better products or services at lower cost, although observers outside Japan may argue that Japanese companies have lost their former splendor due to pursuing multiple value propositions. Japanese companies are extremely conscious of customer satisfaction. While it is clear that a company wins in a severe competition by ensuring a high level of customer satisfaction, in order to do so, it must exercise cost management.

When top managers of Japanese companies are asked about the most important stakeholders for companies, what do you think most of them say? Their answers probably will be *investors, shareholders, customers, employees,* and *communities.* If this question is given to top managers in the United States, their answers will certainly be *shareholders.* What does this difference arise from?

Companies, especially listed companies, are managed with funds provided by shareholders. Therefore, companies must value shareholders as stakeholders. However, to achieve outstanding performance financially, companies must make customers satisfied and draw a higher evaluation and a better act out of customers. To improve customer satisfaction, companies need to be excellent in every process. To make every process excellent, it is important for companies to employ talented people and train them, build better systems, and provide an information system. This is the cause and effect chain shown in "Balanced Scorecard," advocated by Kaplan and Norton. As shown later, the adoption rate of BSC by Japanese companies is extremely low. That is not because Japanese companies that do not adopt BSC do not accept its theory. On the contrary, the logic of BSC is common knowledge in Japanese companies.

Instead, employees are treasured in Japanese companies. I would like to describe the historical background of this feature. The modern history of Japan focused on catching up. In the Edo period (1603–1868) Japan was in international isolation, with few diplomatic relations with other countries. During the Meiji period (1868–1912), the country was far behind Europe and America in terms of knowledge, technology, and social systems. Consequently, Japan rapidly advanced modernization under central government leadership. The phrase "We will make every effort in one body" was often heard in Japan, even after World War II. Japan made a unified effort to regain a rich life under democracy after a disastrous life in bombed ruins.

In modern days, Japan fundamentally focuses on making people's lives rich. Japanese people have roots in agriculture, where people have treasured working in a group for thousands of years. Each person's role was to keep order and play his or her role in the group. The rule of the group was that each person should work for the whole group, and the profits the group earned should be returned to each person. This traditional view forms the basis of Japanese MCSs. All employees working in companies thought that working hard was a contribution to society. For example, Sakichi Toyoda, the founder of Toyota, writes at the beginning of the Five Main Principles of Toyoda (Toyoda Ko-Ryo), "Always be faithful to your duties, thereby contributing to the company and to the overall good" (http://www.toyota-global.com/company/vision_philosophy/guiding_principles. html). This shows that for Toyota, first of all it is important to serve the nation. Also, the phrase, "Always strive to build a homelike atmosphere at work that is warm and friendly" is written in the company's guiding principles. Toyoda persuaded his employees to have a family-like relationship.

Regarding contributing to society, the founder of Panasonic, Kounosuke Matsushita, advocates the philosophy that businesspersons' mission is to supply people with various products as abundantly and cheaply as water. Through this philosophy, the thought that company activities benefited people began to spread throughout the whole company.

Accordingly, Japanese people thought that company employees were a kind of family, that the family made an affluent society in one united body, and finally that it brought them affluence. This history prevented management from thinking that employees were just the labor force, and prevented employees from thinking that a company was just an organization giving pay. Also, as mentioned before, Japanese companies give a high priority to customers. A lot of Japanese people deeply believe that the customer is always right or that the customer is king. On the other hand, U.S. companies probably think that only some targeted customers should be treated as king. Although Japanese companies' view of customers is slightly changing these days, their view that all the customers paying for products or services have the highest priority is still deeply rooted. Compared with U.S. companies, fewer Japanese companies have the view that they should target customers and tailor products or services to their needs.

Viewed in this light, Japanese companies chiefly think of their contribution to society. In other words, their contribution means making an affluent society – that is, improving customers' lives. The development of technology is essential to this mission, including information systems that employees can use and act on; most importantly, Japanese companies need a mission to encourage employees.

I learned that Professor Kaplan and Professor Cooper examined Japanese companies before. Although I do not know whether they learned the basic view of Japanese companies I outlined previously, I can ascertain the same view from their books on BSC and Target Costing. However, there is one differing notion that U.S. companies should focus their efforts on one of the three value propositions.

The basis of Japanese MCSs lies in providing empowerment to front-line employees. However, it would be untrue to say that empowerment is carried out perfectly. Some front-line employees and lower managers do not have much control to change how they work. Nevertheless, such employees should think about how to improve quality, lower costs, and step up the tempo of production. Why do most Japanese employees have such eagerness? What MCSs encourage them to have initiative? I would like to offer some answers of my own to these questions in this book. I will show the present state of Japanese employees, explain what brings about such a state, and attempt to illustrate the Japanese way of thinking.

Incidentally, I do not intend to say that Japanese-style MCSs are always right. Under proper conditions, those MCSs work well in Japanese companies. Inevitably, whether Japanese MCSs work well depends on background in management, especially people's way of thinking about management. A lot of Japanese companies have begun to notice this, and are tailoring Japanese-style MCSs to global management, centering them. Most of the readers of this book will probably want to know about Japanese companies' MCSs and their management style. First, I would like to explain Japanese companies' MCSs and why Japanese companies have such MCSs. That will help you to understand Japanese companies' behaviors.

3. The areas of management control systems in Japan

Some authors classify MCSs into various areas. A detailed way of classifying MCSs is mentioned in Chapter 2 of this book. Here I use the classification by Merchant and Van der Stede (2012). According to them, MCSs can be classified into three main groups: results controls, action controls and personnel controls, and cultural controls. From these three viewpoints, I will explain the features of Japanese companies.

Results controls

The most typical system of results controls is a budgeting system. Under the budgeting system managers at the investment center and the profit center have responsibility for profits, and managers at the cost center have responsibility for costs. When managers attain their budget targets, they are considered to have contributed to the attainment of the organization's objective, and they earn high rewards.

Thus, results controls have a deep connection with a reward system. Employees make efforts to set objectives and achieve them. Companies highly rate employees who can achieve objectives, and give rewards for their good performance. In this case, the objective is often a financial one. Most middle managers and senior managers in particular have financial objectives, as do some lower managers and even some front-line employees.

Results controls in the United States mean that when a manager has high-level objectives and accomplishes them, he/she earns a high reward. These results controls are thought to work very effectively if a company has easy-to-measure financial measures and managers can produce an effect on them. In fact, the pay per performance system (PPP system) in most U.S. companies is structured in this way. On the other hand, although Japanese companies introduce a PPP system partly, they basically adopt a holistic approach of aiming to concentrate on improvement in the whole company's performance, not individual performance.

In *The Japanese Factory* (Abegglen, 1958), James Abegglen cited lifetime employment and seniority-based wages as features of Japanese companies. They maintain lifetime employment, changing seniority-based wages. Each employee's promotion is determined by general judgment based on financial performance, non-financial performance, and evaluations by superiors, colleagues, and subordinates. However, the Japanese pay system is basically pay for skill. It is thought that skills improve with age in Japan, so most companies adopt a compound pay system formed by pay for skill and wages based on job evaluation. That is, Japanese companies not only evaluate an individual's job and skill but also raise wages with years of employment.

Resources for bonuses commonly are divided into three pools. The largest pool is allocated equally to employees based on the entire company's performance. Bonus allocation in Japanese companies depends on financial performance for the previous year and is fixed in the form of several months of employee base salaries. Another pool is allocated based on each division's performance for the previous year, and the other is allocated based on individual performance for the previous year. Although the rate of the last two pools depends on companies, the rate in Japan is much lower than that in the United States. Basically, bonus allocation in Japan is a holistic approach.

A budgeting system has a financial objective, but it does not include an explicit description of how the objective is successfully achieved. Above all, for a profit objective, the logic to describe how the objective is attained is necessary. Balanced Scorecard is a system that describes the logic to execute a strategy and conveys the logic to an organization.

Results controls by budget are a highly effective control system insofar as a company follows some rules. However, even if a company obeys the rules, when top management forces managers to realize an unachievable target and imposes a severe penalty if they cannot reach the target, an extremely big problem arises. Some prime examples are the incidents of accounting fraud at Enron in the United States and Toshiba in Japan. These frauds obviously were caused by the birth of the beyond budgeting model. Extravagant PPP systems often work badly and cause employees to practice fraud. Even Toshiba, which is representative of Japanese companies, is no exception.

Action controls and personnel controls

Action controls clarify what must not be done. According to U.S. literature, many U.S. companies have specific dos and don'ts. In contrast, in Japanese companies the borderline between dos and don'ts is unclear. Of course, each Japanese company has a corporate philosophy, sometimes called Sha-ze, and a code of conduct. Kyocera and Panasonic have famous corporate philosophies and codes of conduct.[1] They are suggestive and obscure in places. In my understanding, these features of corporate philosophy and a code of conduct are influenced by Japanese culture.

Personnel controls have a relationship to employees' tendencies to do the right things. In action controls, specific dos and don'ts are explicit in Sha-ze and a code of conduct. Companies want employees to work according to codes of conduct and often try methods to realize this, mainly through selecting and training employees. Merchant and Van der Stede (2012, pp. 88–89) explain that selection (and placement) is required because companies avoid hiring high-risk individuals. After recruitment, companies train employees to take the right actions. In my opinion, personnel controls are a component of action controls, as is clear from their essence. Thus I bring them together in this book.

Japanese companies value applicants from this viewpoint, whether they fit in corporate culture or not. The recruiting system in Japan seems to be different from that in other countries. The main labor market is for hiring of new graduates because Japanese companies use lifetime employment.[2] Traditionally, Japanese businesspersons have affirmed loyalty to the companies at which they work, and companies hire them for their whole lifetime in return for their loyalty. Companies take in people who have high ability and are an appropriate fit for the company culture.

After recruitment, employees are trained to get the skills needed and to understand their Sha-ze and a code of conduct. This is the same as the training system in United States. However, employees sometimes learn an implicit code of conduct after hours informally. They understand the explicit and implicit rules through formal and informal training.

Cultural controls

In Japan, harmony is valued. The Japanese are originally an agricultural people, and for several thousand years built hierarchies in small villages in which each member contributes to rice production for the whole organization. This history led the Japanese worker to have a strong sense of subordination to an organization, and to work hard for the organization, thus uniting an individual and his or her organization. This national culture underlies Japanese companies' management and also has a great influence on modern management behavior. This organizational unity is a key difference between management control developed in the United States and that used in Japanese companies. Although the variances in U.S. versus Japanese MCSs do not totally result from such cultural differences, this cultural background affecting Japanese MCSs is also discussed in this book.

4. The structure of this book

This book contains 12 chapters in four parts to clarify the features of Japanese MCSs. Part 1 covers the basic concepts of MCSs. The concepts of MCSs developed in the United States and Europe are reviewed in Chapter 2.

Part 2 describes the current status of cost accounting and budgeting systems in Japan. Based on recent research survey, U.S. companies have mainly focused on overhead costs to manage manufacturing costs. On the other hand, Japanese companies have mainly focused on the management of direct manufacturing costs. This is because the production structure in Japan is different from that in the United States. Chapter 3 shows the difference of production circumstances between Japan and the United States and explains the allocation system of overhead costs in Japanese companies based on survey results. Japanese textbooks as well as U.S. textbooks say that overhead costs can be allocated rightly by activity-based costing (ABC). Surely the traditional allocation of overhead costs has some problems. However, most Japanese companies do not use ABC. As far as I know, no scholars point out a big problem with ABC, except the problem that setting a division of cost pools and choosing a cost driver are troublesome. Scholars also do not argue that traditional methods for allocating overhead costs are superior to ABC. So why don't Japanese companies use ABC? I will make the reason clear through the results of my survey.

Chapter 4 shows the challenge to the budgeting system of Japanese companies. Beyond budgeting has been developing since the 1990s, but there are few companies that abolished their budgeting system in Japan. Instead of throwing off their budgeting system, many Japanese companies make improvements to it. In this chapter, I show findings of my research about the budgeting system in Japan.

Part 3 states the difference between Japan and the United States concerning performance management. Chapter 5 explains decentralization in Japanese companies comparing with U.S. companies. Although many Japanese companies have some divisions under a central office, they do not adopt a division system but a functional system as a form of a decentralized system. This has an influence on Japanese MCSs. Chapter 6 describes Balanced Scorecard, which is representative of MCSs developed in recent years. BSC as well as ABC is not adopted by most Japanese companies. In 2000, about 20 companies used BSC. However, most companies do not use it now. According to the examination of Japanese companies made by Japanese studies, the implementation rate of BSC is approximately 10 percent of listed companies. This chapter investigates why Japanese companies do not really adopt BSC and what MCSs in place of BSC they use. Chapter 7 deals with a problem regarding financial measures. U.S. textbooks say that return on investment, return on equity, and economic value added are appropriate as financial measures. However, the usage rate of these measures is not high in Japanese companies. Financial measures still being used in Japanese companies are sales amounts and profits. Although there is a historical background that caused this situation, I believe that the way of thinking of Japanese companies is clearly wrong on this point. Making this historical background clear, this chapter discusses how Japanese companies should change.

Part 4 offers the cases of Japanese companies having characteristic MCSs. Chapter 8 is about the case of Kao, known as a Japanese company that adopted EVA® early. This chapter introduces not the usage of EVA® but instead management of marketing expenses in Kao. The company figures out profit and advertising by deducting manufacturing fixed costs and selling and general administrative costs (except marketing expenses) from contribution margin. It decides how to use marketing expenses depending on the amount of profit and advertising. Chapter 9 introduces transfer pricing in Mitsubishi Electric. There are textbooks explaining transfer pricing, and these textbooks say that companies should not use dual price. Mitsubishi Electric uses the dual pricing system, which makes the best use of a functional system and contributes to the maximization of profits in the whole company.

Chapter 10 through 12 provide topics deeply related to interpretation of the beyond budgeting model. Past studies say that this budgeting system has many problems. Initially the beyond budgeting model proposed abolishing budgets themselves to avoid problems with budgeting systems. The beyond budgeting round table (BBRT) has been trying to find a way to build a better management model rather than to abolish budgets. There are two ways to avoid the problems with budgeting systems. One way is to abolish budgeting systems and build new MCSs centering on BSC as BBRT, as mentioned before. The other is to overcome the problems with budgeting systems and make better use of the system without abandoning it, as shown in Chapter 4. Disco Corporation wholly abolished budgets in 2014 and has adopted the former way. On the other hand, the Japanese company Kyocera has retained a budgeting system named the *master plan*, but has devised some way to make objectives stretch and to achieve them. That is, Kyocera adopts the latter way. Also, it has its own system named the amoeba system. Cooper (1995) calls this system microprofit center, and it often exists in Japanese companies. Chapter 10 and 11 describe the cases of companies that stopped and improved budgets to conduct better MCSs and of companies that tried introducing the concept of BBM without stopping budgets. The final chapter is about the case of Japan Airlines. It relisted in 2011 after going bankrupt in 2009. Kazuo Inamori, who was the founder of Kyocera, was contracted to reestablish JAL and introduced the Kyocera management model into JAL. As a result, it relisted only in two years. Chapter 13 tells the story of how JAL accepted the Kyocera management model and made good use of it.

Notes

1 Konosuke Matsushita is the founder of Panasonic, and his management philosophy remains strong in the company. The business philosophy of Panasonic is "Recognizing our responsibilities as industrialists, we will devote ourselves to the

progress and development of society and the well-being of people through our business activities, thereby enhancing the quality of life throughout the world" (http://www.panasonic.com/global/corporate/management/philosophy.html). Panasonic also has a company creed and seven principles to support corporate philosophy. I will show the Kyocera case in Chapter 11.

2 Recently the situation of hiring has been changing. Companies often hire workers mid-career, and new graduates who enter companies often quit after a few years.

References

Abegglen, J.C. (1958) *The Japanese Factory: Aspects of Its Social Organization*, Glencoe, IL: Free Press.

Anthony, R., J. Dearden, and V.F. Vancil (1965) *Management Control Systems: Cases and Readings*, Homewood, IL: R.D. Irwin.

Anthony, R. and V. Govindarajan (2010) *Management Control Systems*, 12th edition, Boston, MA: McGraw-Hill/Irwin.

Bogsnes, B. (2009) *Implementing Beyond Budgeting: Unlocking the Performance Potential*, Hoboken, NJ: John Wiley & Sons.

Cooper, R. (1995) *When Lean Enterprises Collide: Competing through Confrontation*, Boston, MA: Harvard Business School Press.

Hope, J. and R. Fraser (2005) *Beyond Budgeting: How Manager Can Break Free from the Annual Performance Trap*, Boston, MA: Harvard Business School Press.

Kaplan, R.S. and D.P. Norton (2001) *The Strategy Focused Organization: How Balanced Scorecard Companies Thrive in the New Business Environment*, Boston, MA: Harvard Business School Press.

Kaplan, R.S. and D.P. Norton (2004) *Strategy Maps: Converting Intangible Asset into Tangible Outcome*, Boston, MA: Harvard School Business Press.

Merchant, K. and W.A. Van der Stede (2012) *Management Control Systems: Performance Measurement, Evaluation and Incentives*, 3rd edition, Harlow, UK: Pearson Education Limited.

Neely, A. ed. (2002) *Business Performance Measurement: Theory and Practice*, Cambridge, UK: Cambridge University Press.

Niven, P. (2006) *Balanced Scorecard: Step by Step: Maximizing Performance and Maintaining Result*, 2nd edition, Hoboken, NJ: John Wiley & Sons.

2 Management control systems

Definitions and development

Key learning points

- There are various definitions of management control systems. In this book, the discussions are mainly based on Merchant and Van der Stede (2012).
- What are results controls, action controls, personnel controls, and cultural controls?
- Describe management control systems as systems to implement strategy, as detailed in this chapter.

1. Management accounting and management control systems

Although management accounting has a number of definitions, it is the definition published by the Institute of Management Accountants in 2008 that I often quote (IMA, 2008, p. 1):

> Management accounting is a profession that involves partnering in management decision making, devising planning and performance management systems, and providing expertise in financial reporting and control to assist management in the formulation of an organization's strategy.

Devising performance management is clearly indicated in this definition of management accounting, and it is one of the main roles of management accounting. In fact, since the 1960s performance management accounting and performance measurement have formed one main field of management accounting.

Beyer classifies performance management accounting into three categories: custodial accounting, performance accounting, and decision accounting. According to his definition, performance accounting is the quantitative matching of performance against some plans by organizational responsibility (Beyer, 1963, p. 17), and he says that performance accounting includes all accounting procedures and reports to evaluate an organization's performance. Anthony (1964) and Horngren (1965) support the same definition.

Although Otley – who has achieved much in the field of performance management accounting – does not clarify the definition of performance management, he says that "an organization that is performing well is one that is successfully attaining its objective; in other words, one that is effectively implementing an appropriate strategy" (Otley, 1999, p. 364) and points out that this framework of performance management has been clarified by MCSs.

We will now take a look at the definition of management control (MC) by Anthony, who once defined management control as "the process of assuring that resources are obtained and used effectively and efficiently in the accomplishment of an organization's objective" (Anthony, 1965, p. 245). For Anthony, this includes planning, operating, and measuring and analyzing performance.

The latest definition of MC developed by Anthony is as follows: "Management control is the process by which managers influence other members of the organization to implement the organization's strategies". (Anthony and Govindarajan, 2006, p. 6).

MC includes the following activities (Anthony and Govindarajan, 2006, p. 7):

- Planning what the organization should do
- Coordinating the activities of several parts of the organization
- Communicating information
- Evaluating information
- Deciding what, if any, action should be taken
- Influencing people to change their behavior

Anthony and Govindarajan (2006) classified management activities into management control, strategic formulation, and task control. Task control is intended for the control of tasks; strategic formulation is intended for the control of management policies and goals (Ito, 2009, p. 8); and these are different from management control, which is intended for the control of employees.

Anthony considers MCSs in a relatively narrow sense. He points out that organization structure, human resource management, and culture as well as MCSs are needed in order to implement strategies and raise performance. These four factors link together to work toward implementing a strategy and achieving a target performance as one body.

Although Anthony does not describe clearly what specific tools of MCSs are, viewed from the contents of MCSs, the tools are thought to be budgetary management, transfer pricing, and Balanced Scorecard. These tools have been studied in management accounting and show that MCSs by Anthony have a deep connection with management accounting, particularly performance management.

Budgetary management is a procedure to manage business activities by using budgets. These budgets mean concrete plans in a company's business fields during budgetary periods, formulated as amounts. Budgets include indicating a profit goal during a fixed time period and regulating activities within an organization in order to achieve the goal. After operations are performed based on budgets, the goal and the actual result are calculated, compared, and analyzed, and then the results are reported to top management.

When all managers achieve their budgets, a company is able to achieve its profit goal. And all managers obtain bonuses by achieving their budgets. That is, they make efforts to achieve their budgets through a budgetary management system (and a reward system). Consequently, that leads a company to the achievement of its profit goal. This is an effective system. It is a reward system or program that has a very close connection with all performance management systems, including a budgetary management system. However, when the reward system works too strongly, employees' behaviors may be warped. That is one of the many causes of accounting fraud. Not only companies having strong PPP systems in the United States but also companies deciding rewards through a holistic approach in Japan have this problem. The recent case of Toshiba proves it.[1]

Balanced Scorecard covers a wider span of control than budgets. That is because while budgets cover only financial information, BSC covers non-financial information as well as financial information. The roles of BSC systems (Kaplan and Norton, 2001; 2004; 2008) are to create a road map of a strategy, communicate the road map to all employees, and prompt them to formulate action plans in order to achieve their strategic objectives. This shows the feature of MCSs.

Also, transfer pricing works as an MCS. Transfer price is a price that is set when goods and services are traded between divisions. Transfer price has two functions. One is goal congruence, and the other is performance measurement. Transfer price as MCS is related to the former. When a company has a target as a whole and some divisions make efforts to achieve it together, determining what type of transfer price to set becomes an important problem.

2. Management control systems by Merchant and Van der Stede

MCSs are implemented with the management accounting tools. However, it is not only management accounting tools that have an influence on employees' behaviors. It is clear that organization structure, human resource management, and culture have an influence on employee behavior and support the execution of strategies. Merchant and Van der Stede (2012) discuss MCSs from this perspective. They say that control systems have strategic control and management control, and that the former asks whether organization strategies are valid in changing environments, and that the latter focuses on the execution of strategies and considers employee behavior. They sort the questions as to whether employees behave appropriately further into four questions (Merchant and Van der Stede, 2012, p. 9):

- "Do our employees understand what we expect of them?"
- "Will they pursue the organization's objectives in line with the strategy?"

- "Are they capable of doing a good job?"
- "If the answer to any of these questions is negative, what can be done to solve the management control problem?"

If your answers to the first three questions are all yeses, there is no problem with your organization's MCSs. However, surely there are many cases where one answer or more than one answer is no. In these cases, solutions to the problems are needed.

Merchant and Van der Stede suggest four solutions as follows:

- results control: it focuses on the results produced by managers and employees
- action control: it focuses on the actions taken by managers and employees
- personnel control: it focuses on the types of people employed
- cultural control: it focuses on their shared norms and values

(Merchant and Van der Stede, 2012, p. 17)

Results controls are controls by use of evaluation of employees' performance results and include reward systems such as pay-for-performance. Take a reward system linked to budgetary management systems, for example. By using budgetary management systems, employees' performance results are compared with budgets, and if the results are good, employees can get rewards. Many performance measurement systems regarding managers have the features of results controls. When organizations can define performance dimensions, measure managers' performance clearly, set stretch performance targets, and provide rewards to managers, results controls become effective (Merchant and Van der Stede, 2012, pp. 81–84).

Action controls "involve ensuring that employees perform (do not perform) certain actions known to be beneficial (harmful) to the organization" (Merchant and Van der Stede, 2012, p. 81). Action controls include behavioral constraints, preaction reviews, action accountability, and redundancy (Merchant and Van der Stede, 2012, pp. 81–84).

Personnel controls "build on employees' natural tendencies to control or motivate themselves" and involve selection and placement, training, and job design and resourcing (Merchant and Van der Stede, 2012, p. 88).

Although cultural controls are invisible, they play an important role in management control. Cultural controls are "designed to encourage mutual monitoring; a powerful form of group pressure on individuals who deviate from group norms and values" (Merchant and Van der Stede, 2012, p. 90). Cultural controls often arise when a founder's and senior executives' intentions have penetrated into an organization over the years. Also, cultural controls may be successful experiences shared in an organization. These cultural controls motivate employees to behave as organization desires and to monitor their behaviors mutually.

As pointed out by Merchant and Van der Stede, it is in Japan that cultural controls work most effectively (2012, p. 90). Generally, Japanese employees do not like being different from others in an organization. They like pursuing an organization goal, assimilating to an organization or others in it. Japanese companies have some codes of conduct as a written or unwritten rule. While their employees are willing to keep the codes of conduct, employees will direct rule breakers to keep the codes and in extreme cases employees will exclude rule breakers from organization's activities.

During the period of rapid growth in Japan, it is true that cultural controls worked very effectively in Japanese companies. That is because cultural controls encouraged employees to work together in a body and contributed greatly to economic development in Japan. However, cultural controls in Japanese companies may also have a contrary effect. That is because excessive cultural controls can exclude various ideas and behaviors. Especially in the period of globalization, although diverse products and services need to be offered to diverse markets, forcing uniform thinking and a unified behavior pattern seldom leads to good results. Consequently it is necessary for present Japanese companies to encourage diversity to respond flexibly to customers and markets, while having clear codes of conduct.

MCSs as used by Merchant and Van der Stede clearly covers a broader scope than Anthony's treatment of the concept. Based on a point of view that MCSs have an influence on employee behavior, Merchant and Van der Stede include the whole management system proposed by Anthony. That is to say, MCSs by Merchant and Van der Stede are expanded from Anthony's model as shown in Figure 2.1.

Also, Simons (1994) proposes another type of system. Simons takes four systems (diagnostic control systems, interactive control systems, beliefs systems, and boundary systems) as control systems, and advocates executing MC by these four systems. Diagnostic control systems and interactive control systems are connected with results controls. An organization makes a choice between

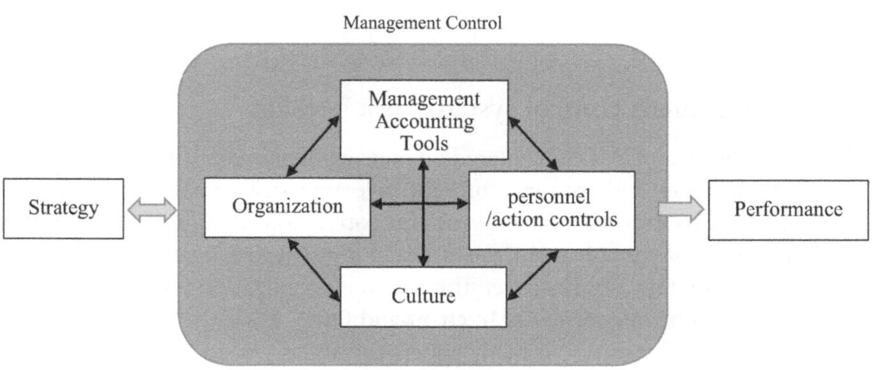

Figure 2.1 Strategic implementing system

diagnostic control systems (feedback systems) and interactive systems (feedforward systems).

Diagnostic control systems are "formal information systems that managers use to monitor organizational outcomes and correct deviations from preset standards of performance" (Simons, 1994, p. 59). This is a normal feedback system. Managers check the difference between actual results and targets. As long as a result exceeds a target, managers do not pay attention to information from this system. Reversely, when a result falls below a target, they start to take immediate action to fill the gap.

In contrast, interactive control systems are "formal information systems managers use to involve themselves regularly and personally in the decision activities of subordinates" (Simons, 1994, p. 95). Managers always make an effort to perceive strategic uncertainties that have a bad influence over or invalidate the existing strategy. Managers should share these strategic uncertainties with their subordinates, because front-line employees sometimes feel some changes in markets first. Thus, interactive control systems focus on adjusting the existing strategy and occasionally creating a new strategy.

These two systems show how management control is conducted. Both diagnostic control systems and interactive control systems are used as results control systems. Interactive control systems are extremely important for MCSs, because the ability to forecast the future is required in turbulent business environments.

Later, Simons extends interactive control systems and defines interactive networks as "the structures and systems that stimulate individuals to gather information and to influence the decisions of others" (Simons, 2005, p. 122). This system is considered as "the horizontal interaction" (Senoo and Yokota, 2015, p. 4) that induces the interaction among different functional divisions in contrast with interactive control systems that are the vertical interaction. In Japan, the concept of the interactive networks, especially shared responsibilities, is critically important. I will show this concept through various Japanese cases.

Beliefs systems indicate the direction of an organization, and cultural controls and boundary systems perform the same functions as action controls and personnel controls.

3. Management control systems as a package

As mentioned before, MCSs, centered on management accounting tools, contain many other factors and are the comprehensive approach of having an influence on employees to execute a strategy by the correlation of those factors. Malmi and Brown (2008) emphasized this point and advocated a package of MCSs. To execute a strategy, "almost everything in the organization is included as part of the overall control systems" (Merchant and Otley, 2007, p. 785). Malmi and Brown conducted research in many papers on MCSs. As a result, they showed the factors of MCSs necessary to execute a strategy, and presented those factors as a package, as shown in Figure 2.2.

<table>
<tr><th colspan="7">Cultural Controls</th></tr>
<tr><td colspan="2">Clans</td><td colspan="3">Values</td><td colspan="2">Symbols</td></tr>
<tr><th colspan="2">Planning</th><th colspan="4">Cybernetic Controls</th><th rowspan="2">Reward and Compensation</th></tr>
<tr><td>Long range planning</td><td>Action planning</td><td>Budgets</td><td>Financial Measurement Systems</td><td>Non Financial Measurement Systems</td><td>Hybrid Measurement Systems</td></tr>
<tr><th colspan="7">Administrative Controls</th></tr>
<tr><td colspan="2">Governance Structure</td><td colspan="3">Organization Structure</td><td colspan="2">Policies and Procedures</td></tr>
</table>

Figure 2.2 Management control systems package
(Malmi and Brown, 2008, p. 291)

I will compare Malmi and Brown's ideas on MCSs with Merchant's model. Cultural controls expressed by Merchant are subdivided into clans, values, and symbols (Malmi and Brown, 2008). Value-based controls are the same as beliefs systems by Simons (1994). Symbol-based controls are shown by Schein (1997) and are visible expressions to build organizational culture. Clan-based controls show that employees are socialized in sub-organizations such as professions and divisions within organizations (Ouchi, 1979).

Next, results controls by Merchant and Van der Stede are subdivided into planning, cybernetic controls, and reward and compensation. Planning and cybernetic controls are management accounting tools themselves, and reward and compensation can be rephrased as "human relation management." Governance structure, and policies and procedures in administrative controls closely resemble action controls. Organization structure is not explicitly included in Merchant's theory.

The phrase "structure follows strategy" is a famous theory shown by Chandler (1962). After that, Ansoff (1979) and Hall and Saias (1980) mentioned that "strategy follows structure." Now Mintzberg's theory (1992) that not a one-way influence but rather a relationship between structure and strategy is reciprocal is gaining widespread acceptance. Anthony and Govindarajan seem to have adopted Mintzberg's assertion and to have included organization structure in Figure 2.1. Although Merchant and Van der Stede do not include organization structure in their books, I will also explain it in this book because the organization structure of Japanese companies is different from that of Europe and the United States.

Thus, the management control systems package by Malmi and Brown contains many factors that have an influence on the implementation of strategies. These factors are important, but not all of the factors are essential to the implementation of strategies. The division of the factors is not clear, and how the relationship between the factors should be formed is obscure. Therefore, this book explains MCSs in Japanese companies based on Figure 2.1, including organization structure, using Merchant and Van der Stede's model with the concept of the interactive network.

Note

1 Toshiba illegally manipulated profits from 2008 to 2014. The amount of illegally overstated profits was reported to be around 160 billion yen.

References

Ansoff, H.I. (1979) *Strategic Management*, London, UK: Palgrave Macmillan.

Anthony, R.N. (1964) *Management Accounting: Text and Cases*, 3rd edition, Homewood, IL: R.D. Irwin.

Anthony, R.N. (1965) *Management Accounting Principle*, Homewood, IL: R.D. Irwin.

Anthony, R.N. and Vijay Govindarajan (2006) *Management Control Systems*, 12th edition, Boston, MA: McGraw-Hill/Irwin.

Beyer, R. (1964) *Profitability Accounting for Planning and Control*, New York, NY: Ronald Press.

Chandler, A.D. Jr. (1962) *Strategy and Structure: Chapters in the History of the American Industrial Enterprise*, Cambridge, MA: MIT Press.

Hall, D.J. and Saias, M.A. (1980) Strategy follows structure! *Strategic Management Journal*, 1(2), 149–163.

Horngren, C.T. (1965) *Accounting for Management Control: An Introduction*, Englewood Cliffs, NJ: Prentice-Hall.

Institute of Management Accountants (2008) *Statements on Management Accounting: Definition of Management Accounting*, Montvale, NJ: Institute of Management Accountants.

Ito, Y. (2009) The basic concept of management accounting, in Kobayashi, Y., Y. Ito, T. Shimizu, and K. Hasegawa (eds.) *Standard Management Accounting*, Chapter 1, Tokyo, Japan: Toyo Keizai Inc., pp. 2–23. Written in Japanese.

Kaplan, R.S. and D.P. Norton (2000) *The Strategy Focused Organization: How Balanced Scorecard Companies Thrive in the New Business Environment*, Boston, MA: Harvard Business School Press.

Kaplan, R.S. and D.P. Norton (2004) *Strategy Maps: Converting Intangible Asset into Tangible Outcomes*, Boston, MA: Harvard Business School Press.

Kaplan, R.S. and D.P. Norton (2008) *Execution Premium: Linking Strategy to Operations for Competitive Advantage*, Boston, MA: Harvard Business School Press.

Malmi, T. and D.A. Brown (2008) Management control systems as a package: Opportunities, challenges, and research directions, *Management Accounting Research*, 19, 287–300.

Merchant, K.A. and D. Otley (2007) A review of the literature on control and accountability, in Chapman, C.S., A.G. Hopwood, M.G. Shields (eds.) *Handbook of Management Accounting Research*, Vol. 2, Amsterdam, The Netherlands: Elsevier, 785–802.

Merchant, K.A. and W.A. Van der Stede (2012) *Management Control Systems: Performance Measurement, Evaluation and Incentives*, 3rd edition, Harlow, UK: Pearson Education Limited.

Mintzberg, H. (1992) *Structure in Fives: Designing Effective Organizations*, Upper Saddle River, NJ: Prentice Hall.

Otley, D. (1999) Performance management: A framework for management control system research, *Management Accounting Research*, 10(4), 363–382.

Ouchi, W. (1979) A conceptual framework for the design of organizational control mechanisms, *Management Science*, 25(9), 833–848.

Schein, E. (1997) *Organizational Culture and Leadership*, San Francisco, CA: Jossey-Bass.

Senoo, T. and E. Yokota (2015) A preliminary study on the effects of transformational leadership on horizontal interactive networks, *Melco Journal of Management Accounting Research*, 8(1), 1–15. Written in Japanese.

Simons, R. (1994) *Levers of Control: How Managers Use Innovative Control Systems to Drive Strategic Renewal*, Boston, MA: Harvard Business School Press.

Simons, R. (2005) *Levers of Organization Design: How Managers Use Accountability Systems for Greater Performance and Commitment*, Boston, MA: Harvard Business School Press.

3 Cost allocation systems

ABC versus Japanese cost accounting innovation

Key learning points

- What are problems in the traditional cost allocation method of manufacturing overhead costs, and how does activity-based costing overcome them?
- How have Japanese companies improved their cost allocation?
- What is the grouping step-down method?

1. The traditional cost allocation method of manufacturing overhead costs

Chapter 3 describes the allocation of manufacturing overhead costs, which is a basic theory in textbooks on cost accounting. The reason why this chapter deals with the allocation is that cost accounting practice in the United States is significantly different from that in Japan. In the United States (and probably in Europe), it is believed that more appropriate costs are derived from the allocation of overhead costs by activity-based costing (ABC) systems than that by traditional department costing systems. While in the United States it is reported that many companies use ABC systems, few Japanese companies use them. Of course, Japanese scholars and businesspersons also understand the merits of ABC systems, but the reason why few Japanese companies use ABC systems is probably that they have unique cost allocation systems. This chapter provides an overview of traditional cost allocation systems and ABC systems, and explains how hybrid cost allocation systems mix both these systems in Japanese companies.

The allocation of overhead costs is a topic that has been discussed for a long time. In the period of a high percentage of direct costs to manufacturing costs, this was not a big problem, because charging direct costs to specific products is very easy. However, as automated manufacturing systems have developed, the ratio of overhead costs to manufacturing costs has increased. Therefore, the results of cost accounting using the plant-wide allocation rate, which is the simplest method, have become less reliable. This is because with the upsizing of factories and the establishment of many operating and support departments, these types of overhead costs increased, and their cost behaviors were considerably

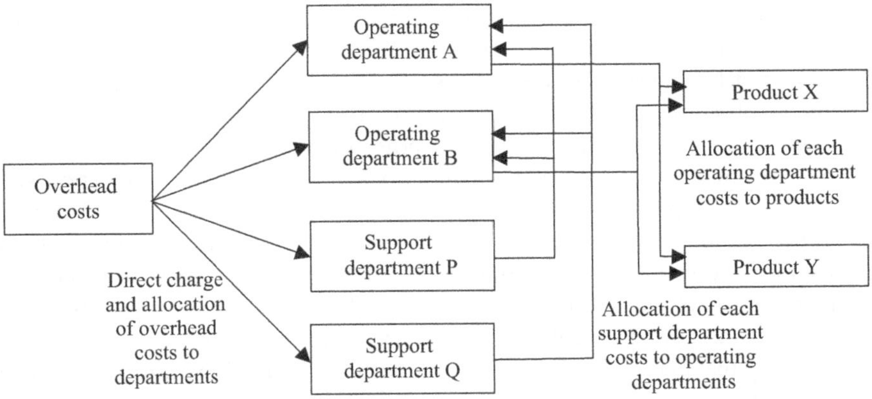

Figure 3.1 Allocation system of overhead costs by using the direct method

different. When cost behaviors are different, cost drivers for allocation should be naturally different. Accordingly, it is clear that using only one allocation rate is an inappropriate method.

In order to overcome this problem, a department costing system was invented. In this system, overhead costs are assigned to operating departments and support departments, and costs in each support department are allocated to operating departments and other support departments. At this stage, we can use three methods: a direct method, a step-down method, and a reciprocal method. Figure 3.1 shows the allocation of overhead costs to two products, X and Y, by using the direct method.[1]

First, overhead costs are divided into two categories: direct departmental overhead costs and indirect departmental overhead costs. Direct departmental overhead costs are charged, and indirect departmental overhead costs are allocated to departments. Second, costs in each support department (the sum of charged and allocated overhead costs) are allocated to operating departments by using a specific cost allocation rate. It is calculated by dividing support-department costs by the total amount of services delivered by the support department. Finally, costs in each operating department (the sum of charged and allocated overhead costs and allocated support-department costs) are allocated to two products.

Each support department offers services to operating departments, and each operating department produces products. Department costing systems can rightly reflect this production flow in cost accounting.

2. The development of activity-based costing

Compared with the former allocation model, a department costing system can conduct cost accounting more correctly. However, it has some problems under the present production environment.

First, with accelerating innovation in production automation, direct labor decreases and some factories have little direct labor. As mentioned before, the complication of production processes and an increase in overhead costs associated with it led department costing systems to the development, but the development of computer-integrated manufacturing and flexible manufacturing systems steadily increased the rate of overhead costs.

Second, market-oriented management considerably changed production systems. It is often pointed out that supplying a large amount of the same products by mass production was needed before. However, with the diverse needs of consumers, companies must manufacture many kinds of products to meet consumers' needs by flexible production plans. Moreover, it is necessary to grasp their needs as soon as possible, manufacture products adaptable to their needs in a timely manner, and deliver them to consumers with short lead time. These points affected product costs. Cooper and Kaplan (1988) pointed out that due to a great change in production circumstances since the 1980s, costs were distortedly calculated by department costing systems, so they proposed activity-based costing (ABC).

ABC is a cost accounting system responding to new production circumstances. In ABC, each activity is a basic cost object (a cost pool) and overhead costs are assigned to each activity. Then the costs assigned to each activity are allocated to the final cost objects such as products, services, and customers by using cost drivers, which are the used amount of the activities (see Figure 3.2).

Activities are items to pool resources consumed in producing products and services – for example, cutting metal, polishing material, assembling parts included in operating departments, and designing products, moving materials, and inspecting finished goods are included in support departments. By producing many kinds of products flexibly, production processes changed and the role of support departments to support operating departments became significantly important.

An example of a change in production processes is an increase in setup. High-mix, low-volume production makes a factory manufacture many types of products at low lot size. It invites frequent setup activities. Tens of thousands of products per setup could be produced before, but there are some cases where only thousands or hundreds of products can be produced lately. Even though lot size is 10,000, 100, or even only one unit, given that setup costs per setup are not so different, the lower the lot size is, the higher setup costs spent on products per unit are. This is the first change.

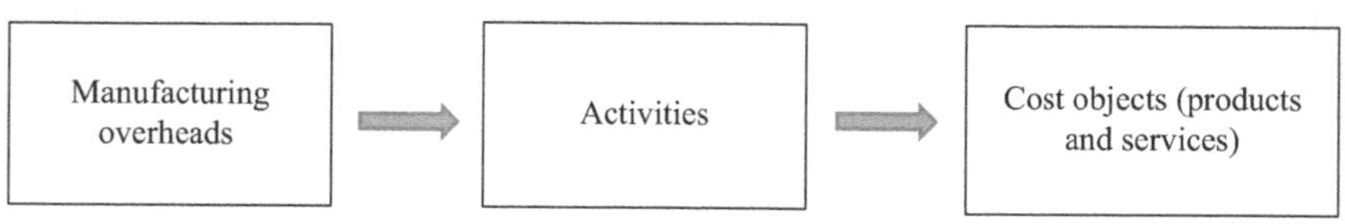

Figure 3.2 Cost flow in ABC systems

Next I will explain how the role of support departments became important. As mentioned previously, when we try to efficiently manufacture many types of products at low lot size – in other words, when production processes become complicated – the activities of the scheduling products department inevitably increase, and the same applies to the moving activity and the delivering activity of material departments.

These two points cause troubles in traditional department costing systems. That is because costs of activities in support departments allocated to an operating department are allocated to products or services by an operating department's volume – that is, direct hours or machinery hours consumed by each product or service. In many cases, costs of activities in support departments are not generated by operating department's volume. Therefore, using other cost drivers that generate their costs, the costs must be allocated to products or services.

Based on the previous theory, Figure 3.3 shows a calculating process of ABC. At first, indirect material costs, indirect labor costs, and indirect expenses are assigned to activities or cost pools. They are activity costs. Next, they are allocated to products by using cost drivers. For example, activity costs of delivery are allocated by the number of parts and activity costs of assembling setup are allocated by setup hours and so on.

According to the theory of ABC systems, costs are incurred when activity is consumed. Because cost drivers (cost-allocation bases) are directly related to consuming activity in ABC systems, costs of each activity are allocated more suitably to cost objects than in traditional department costing systems that allocate many types of overheads by only one cost-allocation base.

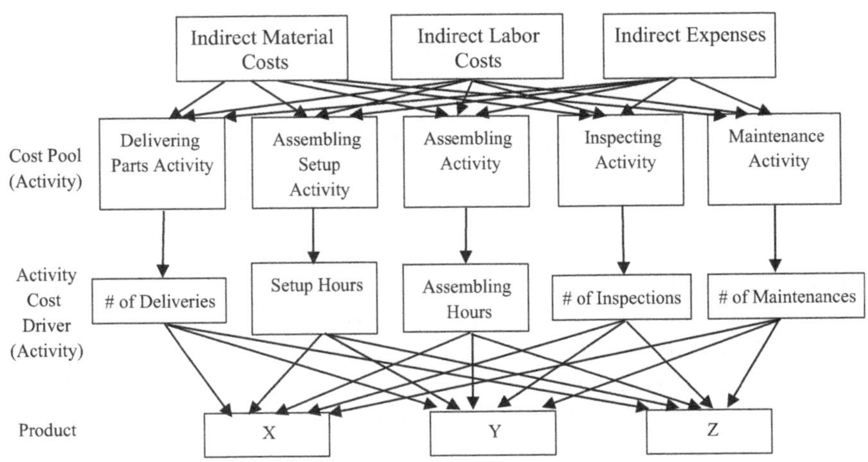

Figure 3.3 The process of ABC systems

3. Cost hierarchies

Activities are classified by cost hierarchy dimensions. Cooper (1990) divided activities into four categories: unit-level, batch-level, product-sustaining, and facility-sustaining activities.

Unit-level activities are the activities that are needed to make a unit of product or service. Assembling body, cutting materials, and painting are typical examples of unit-level activities.

Batch-level activities are the activities that are needed to operate a batch. Preparing a machine to change setups is a typical example of batch-level activities.

Product-sustaining activities are the activities that are needed to support each product or service, not production departments. Designing products and delivering materials for a specific product are typical examples of product-sustaining activities.

Facility-sustaining activities are the activities that are needed for general administration.

Thus, activities are classified into four categories and costs accumulated in each activity are activity costs. That is, unit-level costs are the costs incurred by using unit-level activities. Because the cost driver of unit-level costs is volume of each activity, the way of allocating to products is not different from that in traditional costing. However, the cost driver of batch-level costs is the number of batch or setup hours, and the cost driver of product-sustaining costs is labor hours for design or the frequency of delivery of materials. Consequently, the results by ABC systems are different from those by traditional department costing systems. Finally, facility-sustaining costs are the costs for general administration in a factory and cannot be traced to each product. It is difficult or impossible to find a proper cause-and-effect relationship between costs and a cost-allocation base. Therefore, the total amount of facility-sustaining costs as period costs is deducted from current revenues in ABC systems.

4. Current status of Japanese cost allocation system

No one questions that ABC systems are more effective than department costing systems under the current manufacturing circumstances. Still, few Japanese manufacturers have adopted ABC systems. The Japan Accounting Association (1999) did a mail-in survey of companies listed on the first section of the Tokyo Stock Market in 1998. According to this survey, only 22 companies (approximately 6.7 percent) of 330 responding companies were conducting ABC/ABM. Also, according to a cross-national survey done by Bhimani et al. (2007), the percentage of Japanese companies using ABC in the majority of units was 13.4 percent, and the percentage of Japanese companies using ABC across units was 6.1 percent. This survey was made in Canada, France, Germany, Italy, the United Kingdom, the United States, and Japan, and the average for each of those countries except Japan ranged from 29.2 percent to 44 percent. While the percentage of perceiving potential usefulness of ABC in Japanese companies was 86.3 percent, the rate of usage of ABC in Japanese companies was clearly much lower than that in other countries.

Before examining the reason, I will overview the result of a survey of overhead cost allocation systems in Japanese companies.

In 2010 I mailed survey questionnaires to 1,283 listed companies in Japan, with 200 companies responding. The results are shown in the following section. Unless otherwise specifically noted, the statistical figures are the results of this research.

5. The current ratio of overhead costs to manufacturing costs

Table 3.1 indicates the current ratio of overhead costs to manufacturing costs. Over 50 percent of companies had a ratio under 30 percent, and about 30 percent of companies had a ratio between 30 percent and 50 percent. That is, the ratio of overhead costs to manufacturing costs under 50 percent comes to around 80 percent. According to data classified by industry, the metal/nonferrous metal industry (56.3 percent) and the automobile/auto parts industry (52.9 percent) show relatively high percentages.

Additionally, I questioned those companies about the ratio during the past 20 years and in the future. As a result, 31 percent of companies answered that the ratio increased, and 15 percent of companies answered that the ratio will increase.

This point is different from the opinion in the United States that a marked increase in overhead costs created ABC. It is said that the rate of overhead costs in Japanese companies has been relatively lower than that in U.S. companies. Japanese companies have been trying to reduce overhead costs directly. They consider that the allocation of overhead costs is just fiction or a story, only to allocate costs to each product. For them, reducing overhead costs is much more important than allocating them accurately. For example, Japanese companies have been making an effort to shorten setup hours. It took a few hours for car manufacturers to change a mold in a press process 20 years ago, but now it

Table 3.1 The current ratio of overhead costs to manufacturing costs

1. Under 30%	101	50.5%
2. 30%~50%	57	28.5%
3. 50%~70%	17	8.5%
4. Over 70%	4	2.0%
N.A.	21	10.5%
Total	200	100.0%

(Shimizu, 2014, p. 64)

takes only a few minutes. It is clear that this effort decreased setup costs. Many Japanese companies have been trying to cut overhead costs themselves, not to devise a new and sophisticated cost accounting system.

Recently, manufacturers make use of a temporary agency to cut costs of plant workers who work for indirect operation. Some companies outsource the work of material departments. Conventionally manufacturers inspected and sorted materials. Now they may outsource this work or let suppliers inspect and sort when they deliver materials. I have seen many manufacturers cut overhead costs by outsourcing supporting activities or optimizing supply chain mechanics.

There is another reason why the ratio of overhead costs to manufacturing costs is low in Japan. It is the vertical supplier system in the assembly industry. Assemblers in the United States manufacture parts in-house, but in Japan they purchase most parts from suppliers. The more manufacturing department parts there are, the more support departments there are. As a result, overhead costs increase. On the other hand, when parts are purchased from suppliers, all the costs are direct material costs.

Assume that a manufacturer makes a product A by processing a part P. Company X makes the part P in-house, but Company Y purchases it from a supplier. Cost structures of both Companies X and Y are shown in Figure 3.4.

Because Company X manufactures a part P in-house, overhead costs of both production and processing of P are incurred. Moreover, activities to support and adjust both production and processing of P are needed, and overhead costs increase.

In contrast, because Company Y purchases part P from a supplier, the price of part P is direct materials in Company Y, and overhead costs of only processing of part P are needed. The price of P includes the profits of a supplier, and it may seem that the price of P in Company Y is higher than the cost of P in Company X. However, it is not correct. A supplier, who is a specialist in the production of part P, probably produces it much more efficiently than an assembler.

For these reasons, Japanese companies have focused on the calculation and control of manufacturing direct costs, not overhead costs. This led Japanese companies to create target costing.[2]

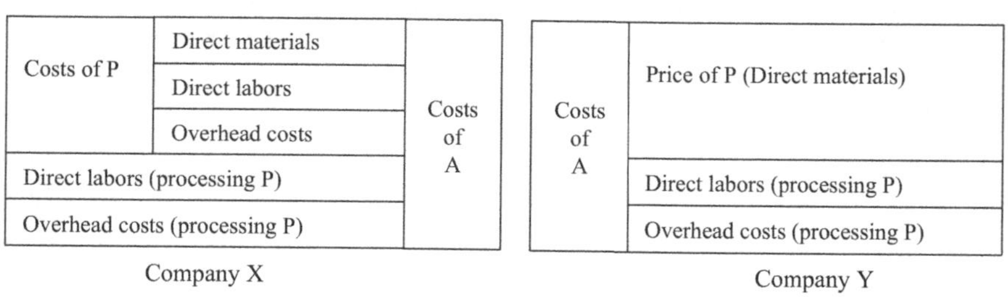

Figure 3.4 Cost structure

6. Direct method, step-down method, or reciprocal method?

As is well known, there are two types of cost departments: operating departments (production departments) and support departments (service departments). Operating departments make products or parts, and support departments assist other departments by delivering their services. Moreover, support departments are sometimes classified into two types: a department giving specific services to operating and other support departments, such as a power department, a material department, and an information system department, and a department managing a factory as a whole, such as a plant management department.

Basically, costs of a support department should be allocated to operating departments and other support departments when they use the services from the support department. As mentioned before, there are three methods for allocating support-department costs: a direct method, a step-down method, and a reciprocal method. They are regulations in the Cost Accounting Standards (CAS)[3] in Japan.

The direct method is simple and easy to calculate. However, it can lack the accuracy of the result because it does not take account of delivering services among support departments. In contrast, the reciprocal method recognizes all services delivered among support departments. Thus, it is said that the result of allocation with this method is correct. Under the step-down method, costs of some support departments are allocated to other support departments. To use this method, we need to rank support departments by some criteria. The costs should be allocated from higher ranked support departments to lower ranked ones, but the opposite flow never happens. This is the product of a compromise between accuracy and easiness.

According to informal surveys of some Japanese manufacturers, in addition to these three methods, I found that another one, a grouping step-down method, was used by many companies.

In the grouping step-down method, support departments are divided into two groups. Group A, the support department R in Figure 3.5, clearly delivers its services to operating departments and other support departments, such as a

Table 3.2 Allocation methods

Direct method	90	55.5%
Step-down method	13	8.0%
Grouping step-down method	39	24.1%
Reciprocal method	16	9.9%
N.A.	4	2.5%
Total	162	100.0%

(Shimizu, 2014, p. 72)

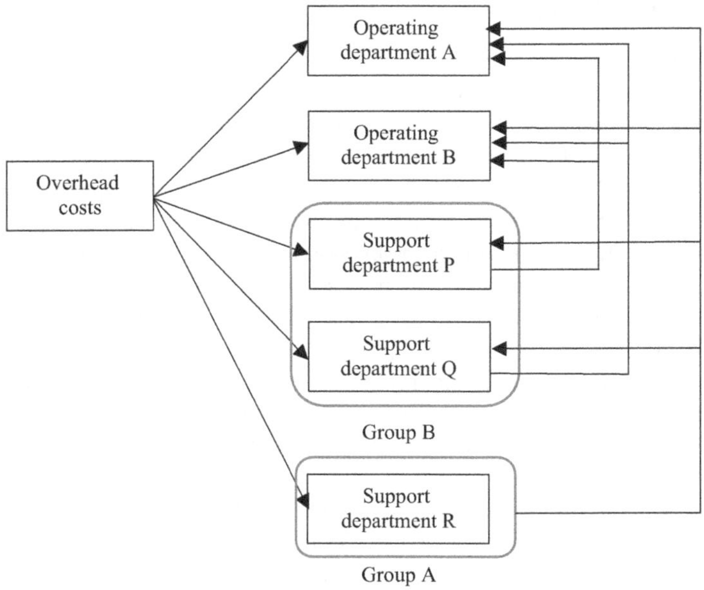

Figure 3.5 Grouping step-down method (1)

plant management department and a power department. Group B, supports departments P and Q in Figure 3.5, and does not deliver or hardly delivers their services to other support departments. Their services are used only by operating departments. Costs of the support department R in group A are allocated to operating departments and other support departments in group B. And costs of support departments in group B are allocated only to operating departments.

A total of 55.5 percent of the respondents use the direct method (see Table 3.2). The second largest category is "the grouping step-down method." This method is simpler than the step-down method. Support departments are set to deliver their services to operating departments. Thus, if the portion of services delivered to other support departments in a support department is very small, companies do not need to reflect this flow in cost allocation.

7. Special support departments and cost allocation by CAS in Japan

CAS directs manufacturers to use department cost systems in job costing systems. 73.5 percent of the respondents using job costing systems and process costing systems adopt department cost systems at all their factories. In contrast, the rate of the companies that do not adopt those systems is 15.0 percent. This is not because those companies are small in scale. As the machine industry conducting built-to-order manufacturing, when many plant workers work together in a production line, there can be little need for department costing.

However, there are a few exceptions to the allocation of support department costs. More specifically, a few regulations in CAS give permission to allocate support department costs directly to products, not to operating departments and other support departments.

The classification of operating departments versus support ones is relative. Large-scale support departments such as a power department often exceed operating departments in equipment and the number of staff. Therefore, CAS 16–2 says that large-scale support departments can be regarded as operating departments. 67.2 percent of the companies using department cost systems have this type of support department. The costs of these support departments are allocated to products when these departments are treated as operating departments.

In addition to CAS 16–2, 18–2 says that support department costs can be allocated directly to products, if needed. In this case, companies can allocate support-department costs to products even though the scale is not so large. According to my research, 25.3 percent of respondents make use of this regulation.

8. Japanese companies practices for allocating support department costs

As mentioned earlier, few Japanese companies introduce ABC systems, even though neither academicians nor practitioners take a position against ABC systems. Why do Japanese companies not apply ABC systems? Do they have no alternative but to use an outdated cost accounting system because they do not have any knowledge and skill to introduce and master ABC systems? The answer I found is emphatically "no." Japanese companies have been devising a unique cost-allocation system, identifying overhead costs as direct costs as far as possible, and using CAS 16–2 and 18–2 to improve the problem with the traditional cost-allocation system.

Japanese companies have the classification of overhead costs similar to that in ABC systems. For example, a Japanese car manufacturer has three categories of support departments:

1 There is a support department in an operating department, and this support department delivers its services to a particular operating department. Costs of some activities in this support department are recognized as unit-level activity costs because those activities are strongly related to the activities of the operating department. Thus, there is no problem to allocate the costs by the volume of this operating department, because this volume is an appropriate cost driver even in ABC systems. However, when activities relate to a specific product, not to production volume, their costs are recognized as product-sustaining activity costs.

2 There are some support departments that deliver their services to some operating departments. These services are classified into two types. One includes services produced mainly to support operating departments' activities, such as a power department and a maintaining equipment department. Costs of these services are unit-level activity costs. The other includes services produced mainly to support a specific product, such as investigating complete products and delivering materials. Costs of these services are product-sustaining activity costs.
3 There are some plant-wide management departments. Costs of these departments are facility-sustaining activity costs.
4 As to batch-level activities, setup activities are measured as direct labor hours. 67.3 percent of the respondents measure setup time for each product. Therefore, setup costs can be treated as "direct costs" in these companies. They can charge setup costs to products.

This case is merely a company's approach. However, I have seen many companies that classify their support departments into two or three groups, as this car manufacturer does.

Although the costs are classified, if support department costs are allocated to operating departments, the result of cost accounting might be distorted. Still, many Japanese companies are pursuing the appropriate allocation of overhead costs by developing a hybrid system of a grouping step-down method and CAS 16–2/18–2.

Figure 3.6 shows the innovative allocation system in Japanese companies developed as a substitute for ABC systems. Support department P supplies its

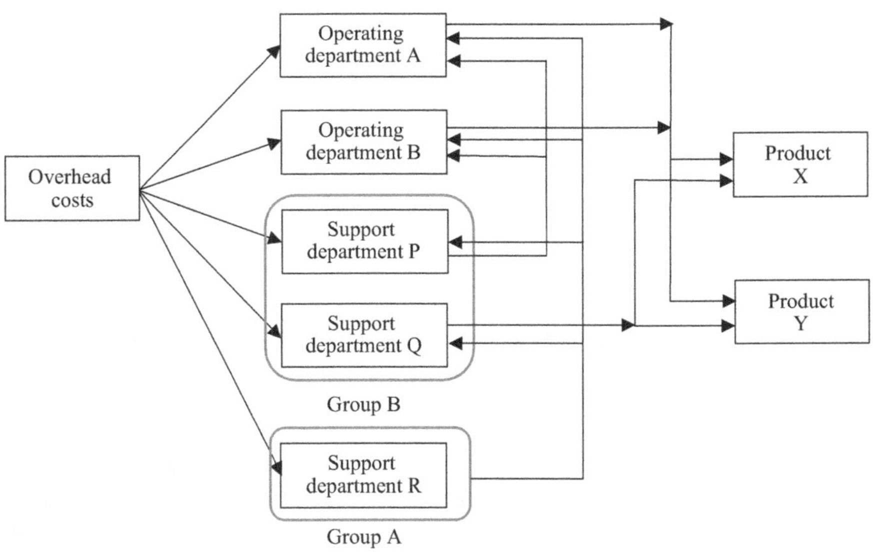

Figure 3.6 Grouping step-down method (2)

services mainly to operating departments. Support department Q supplies them to products, not operating departments. Support department R supplies them to all other departments. Of course, support departments are sometimes integrated into a group as shown in Figure 3.5. I will now explain the assumption that each group has only one department. Costs of the support department R are allocated to operating departments and support departments P and Q, or all other departments (groups), and the cost-allocation base is the amount of service. In the support department P, the sum of costs allocated from R and costs of the department P itself is allocated to operating departments. In the support department Q, the sum of costs allocated from R and costs of the department Q itself is allocated to products X and Y, not operating departments.

This method is a kind of hybrid of traditional department cost systems and ABC systems, and allows us to reflect the mutual services provided among departments in cost accounting and to allocate the product-sustaining activity costs to products in order to avoid distortions in traditional cost allocation systems.

ABC systems were developed to overcome problems with traditional department costing systems. These problems arise from the existence of batch-level activity costs and product-sustaining activity costs. They are unrelated to the volume of operating departments. Thus, these costs need a suitable cost-allocation base. ABC systems improve this point by dividing operating and support departments into many small activities and preparing a suitable cost driver of the allocation of each activity cost. Costs of facility-sustaining activities may be treated as period costs because they have no cause-and-effect relationship with making products (Horngren et al., 2012, p. 149).[4]

9. The reason why many Japanese companies do not introduce ABC systems

ABC systems do not reflect services delivered from support departments to operating departments in cost accounting. In these systems, we assume that products directly consume every service. However, the support departments such as a power department clearly provide power to other departments. Consequently, it is inadequate to ignore the relationship among departments. In fact, when a factory tries to find how much power each unit of product consumes, this factory measures power used by each operating department, which processes a product at first, and after that, it measures how much power a product consumes in each operating department. This process is nothing but the procedure of department costing systems.

Therefore, costs of support departments that clearly provide their services to other departments should be allocated to these departments (the support departments P and R in Figure 3.6), and costs of support departments that clearly provide their services to products should be allocated to these products (the support department Q). Costs of batch-level activities, such as setup, can be rationally allocated to products as long as the setup time is measured. As shown earlier, over two-thirds of Japanese companies measure setup time by the product.

Companies can collect all the data indicated and allocate overhead costs in department costing systems. Therefore, in the hybrid cost allocation system, companies can avoid difficulties with ABC systems because they do not need to gather additional data. As mentioned previously, the reason why Japanese companies do not use ABC systems is the existence of the hybrid cost allocation system as well as the low rate of overhead costs.

In my opinion, companies can introduce this hybrid cost allocation system much more easily than ABC systems, to improve problems inherent in the traditional department costing systems.

10. Dual-rate method

In this section, I explain a dual-rate method of allocating support department costs. In the dual-rate method, variable costs and fixed costs are allocated by different cost-allocation bases. Normally a used amount of services is chosen as a cost-allocation base, or a cost driver. However, the cost-allocation bases of a variable cost and a fixed cost should be different because cost behavior of each cost is different. Variable costs are allocated by the used amount of services. On the other hand, fixed costs should be allocated by the budget base.

Once the budgeted production volume in a company is decided, operating departments calculate their requirements of the service volume from each support department. Each support department prepares its volume based on the sum of service requirements from operating departments. Therefore, fixed costs in a support department are unrelated to the used amount of services. Fixed costs should be allocated based on the requirements of the service volume in budgets. According to my research, 29.0 percent of the respondents use the dual-rate method, as shown in Table 3.3.

Table 3.3 Dual-rate method or single-rate method?

Dual-rate method	47	29.0%
Single-rate method	113	69.8%
N.A.	2	1.2%
Total	162	100.0%

(Shimizu, 2014, p. 72)

11. Allocating operating department costs to products

The hybrid cost-allocation system mainly uses the structure of department costing systems. Costs accumulated in operating departments are allocated to products. Japanese companies use their ingenuity to do it. Generally, to allocate operating department costs to products, companies calculate the allocation rate by dividing the costs of an operating department by its volume (an allocation base) – for example, direct labor hours (DLH) or machinery hours (MH) – and multiplying this allocation rate by the volume consumed by each product. Table 3.4 shows what kind of allocation base job costing companies use. According to my research, there are 89 companies using the job costing system.

In this table, "single base" is not equal to "single-rate" in Section 10. A dual rate means different cost-allocation bases are applied to variable costs and fixed costs. On the other hand, in Table 3.4 costs are not divided into variable and fixed costs. It shows one or more than one allocation base is applied to total costs.

Fifty-seven companies use the single base and most of them use direct labor hours as an allocation base. However, 10 companies use non-hour allocation bases for different factories or processes. Alternatively, 28 companies assign operating department costs to some cost pools and apply different cost-allocation bases to these cost pools. Including 8 companies which use the combination of DLH, MH, and other bases, 28 companies use more than one allocation base. Other allocation bases are not time-based but quantity-based, such as weights, dimensions, or quantity of products. It suggests that there are still many cost factors influenced by quantity.

In any cases, companies have been using these multi-allocation bases for years. This suggests that Japanese companies have been pursuing better methods of allocating overhead costs.

Although there is only one case, a chemical company uses a very interesting method of allocating operating department costs to products. It divides operating department costs into two categories: variable costs and fixed costs. Variable costs are allocated to products by the used amount of volume such as

Table 3.4 Allocation bases of operating department costs

Single base (multiple answers)			*Multi-base*				
Direct labor hours	*Machinery hours*	*Other base*	*DLH+ MH+ others*	*DLH+ others*	*MH+ others*	*DLH+ MH*	*Other combination*
48	11	12	7	8	1	8	4

(Shimizu, 2014, p. 73)

DLH or MH, and budgeted fixed costs are charged to each product. Although fixed costs per unit of product change as the production volume of this product changes in this allocation method, a product can cover all of the budgeted fixed costs. A normal dual-rate method is used to allocate support department costs, but this practice is a dual-rate method of allocating "operating department costs." This is a new method of an allocation system, and it may be applicable to ABC systems.

Notes

1 The step-down method and the reciprocal method are always explained in cost accounting textbooks. For more information, see Horngren et al. (2012, pp. 551–555).
2 Target costing is not included in this book because there are many books and papers that introduce target costing. For more information, see Cooper and Slagmulder (1997; 1999) and Monden (1995).
3 The Japanese Cost Accounting Standards (CAS) were set in 1962. Now they are not enforceable by any court, but most of the manufacturers calculate manufacturing costs based on CAS. Some academicians claim that CAS is too outdated because it was set more than 60 years ago. However, in my opinion, in totality it is acceptable and some of the contents may be very useful even now.
4 Japanese companies cannot treat the costs of facility-sustaining activities as period costs because CAS in Japan requires an absorption costing system.

References

Bhimani, A., M. Gosselin, M. Ncube, and H. Okano (2007) Activity-based costing: How far have we come internationally? *Cost Management*, 21(3), 12–17.

Cooper, R. (1990) Cost classifications in unit-based and activity-based manufacturing cost systems, *Journal of Cost Management*, Fall, 4–14.

Cooper, R. and R.S. Kaplan (1988) Measure costs right: Make the right decisions, *Harvard Business Review*, 66(5), 96–103.

Cooper, R. and R. Slagmulder (1997) *Target Costing and Value Engineering*, Portland, OR: Productivity.

Cooper, R. and R. Slagmulder (1999) *Supply Chain Development for the Lean Enterprise: Interorganizational Cost Management*, Portland, OR: Productivity.

Horngren, T.H., S.M. Datar, and M. Rajan (2012) *Cost Accounting: A Managerial Emphasis*, 14th edition, Upper Saddle River, NJ: Prentice Hall.

Japan Accounting Association, Special Study Group (1999) *The Research of the Theory and Practice of ABC and ABM*, Japan Accounting Association.

Monden, Y. (1995) *Cost Reduction Systems: Target Costing and Kaizen Costing*, Portland, OR: Productivity.

Shimizu, T. (2014) *Cost Accounting Available to Practitioners*, Tokyo, Japan: Chuokeizai-sha Inc. Written in Japanese.

4 A challenge to better budgeting in Japanese companies

Key learning points

- Do Japanese companies feel that their budgeting systems have significant problems?
- If not, how do they make improvements to their budgeting systems?

1. Introduction

I have proposed that key performance indicator (KPI) forecast management is based on the idea that problems with budgeting systems can be overcome by introducing the essence of the beyond budgeting model (BBM) into budgeting systems without abolishing budgets (Shimizu, 2013). As explained in detail in Chapter 10, BBM is a model of thinking that says that because defects in budgeting systems are unacceptable, those systems should be abolished and a new management system, BBM, should be developed. On the other hand, the point of the KPI forecast management model is to adopt 3 of 12 principles in BBM (Bogsnes, 2009): the relative targets, the holistic approach to rewards, and the continuous planning by using a rolling forecast.

Kyocera Corporation and Disco Corporation were introduced as examples of Japanese companies abolishing budgets and adopting those principles, but most Japanese companies keep using budgeting systems. For example, according to research (Yokota et al., 2012), 259 of 262 respondents surveyed use budgeting systems (98.9 percent). Why do those companies use budgeting systems if there are unacceptable defects in them as claimed in BBM?

Also, it is not only in Japan but also in the United States and Canada that budgeting systems are still used, and it is reported that many of the companies there do not have strong dissatisfaction with budgets (Libby and Lindsay, 2010).

Which of these contrary ideas is correct, beyond budgeting or budgeting systems? According to recent information on corporate websites, the number of companies participating in the beyond budgeting round table has not increased. Many companies worldwide are unwilling to adopt extreme BBM, and Japan is no exception. Moreover, BBRT seems to backpedal slightly because it does not seem to focus on the abolishment of budgeting systems.

My answer to this question is that companies can overcome problems associated with budgeting systems. However, little attention has been given to how to overcome the problems. To make this clear, I did research by sending a questionnaire to Japanese companies. The results are as follows.

2. Survey

This survey was conducted from February to March 2015 and designed for 1,863 Japanese companies listed on the first section of the Tokyo Stock Exchange (TSE). I also collected data from 187 companies listed on TSE Mothers to compare the results of large and mature companies with those of relatively small and start-up companies. The number of respondents was 192 in the first section and 17 in Mothers, a response rate of 10.3 percent and 9.1 percent, respectively.

Table 4.1 is a list by type of industry of the respondents. In regard to Mothers companies, because the respondents are low in number and include too many non-manufacturing companies, especially service companies, attention should be given to the fact that this list does not show the features of this

Table 4.1 The type of industry of the respondents

	FSCs	*MCs*		*FSCs*	*MCs*
Food	7		Construction	15	
Textile	2		Trading company	13	
Pulp and paper	2		Retail	18	3
Chemical	17		Bank	4	
Pharma	4	1	Securities	1	
Oil	2		Insurance	0	1
Rubber	1		Other financial business	6	
Ceramic	2		Real estate	6	
Steel	5		Railroad and bus	1	
Non-ferrous metals and metals	7		Land transportation	1	
Industrial machines	13		Air transportation	2	
Electric equipment	25		Warehousing	2	
Shipbuilding	1		Telecommunication	2	
Automobiles/parts of automobiles	5		Gas	1	
Precision machines	6		Service	19	11
Other manufacturing	2	1	Total of non-manufacturing industries	91	15
Total of manufacturing industries	101	2	All industries	192	17

category sufficiently. In Table 4.1, "companies listed on the first section of TSE" are abbreviated to FSCs and "companies listed on TSE Mothers" are MCs.

3. Do companies use budgetary management or not?

It is practically impossible for companies to exercise management without financial management systems. Even the companies adopting the beyond budgeting model have some financial management systems. I asked companies a question to confirm whether they had some financial management systems regardless of the name of budgets (see Table 4.2). As a result, it became clear that most of the companies had financial planning, coordinating, and control systems. However, there were two FSCs having no such system. On the basis of past experience, although I know that there are certain companies with no budgeting function, I need to pursue research further on what management systems those companies have. More MCs do not use the term *budgeting*, and start-up companies tend to be unconcerned with using the tools of traditional management accounting.

4. Problems with budgeting systems

The purpose of this question is to investigate what Japanese companies think about problems with budgets, pointed out by many academicians as well as advocators of beyond budgeting. As mentioned previously, some surveys show that companies do not really recognize problems with budgeting systems.

The result of this survey is almost the same as that of the previous survey; 1 and 5 in Table 4.3 are the points at issue in FSCs.

The reason 1 and 5 indicate a big difference in results between FSCs and MCs can be considered as follows: 1 seems to be related to scale. The larger the business is in scale, the more complicated the processes of budget drafting. Concerning 5, it can be supposed that MCs are longer-term-oriented – that is, MCs aim at achieving success in mid-term performance, not current performance. Although the reason for these answers is discussed later, the level of satisfaction with budgeting systems is examined by asking the following question.

Table 4.2 Do companies use budgetary management or not?

	FSCs		*MCs*	
1 Use budgeting management	173	90.1%	12	75.0%
2 Do not use the term "budgeting management" but have financial planning, coordinating, and control systems the same as budgeting systems.	17	8.9%	4	25.0%
3 Do not have budgeting systems. No alternative approach to budgeting systems that implement planning, coordinating, and control.	2	1.0%	0	0%
Total	192		16	

Table 4.3 Problems with budgeting systems (5: strongly agree, 4: agree, 3: neutral, 2: disagree, 1: strongly disagree)

		FSCs		*MCs*	
1 Too many processes and great cost for budgeting systems	5	28	14.6%	0	0.0%
	4	81	42.2%	4	23.5%
	3	41	21.4%	8	47.1%
	2	37	19.3%	5	29.4%
	1	5	2.6%	0	0.0%
	AVG	3.469		2.941	
2 Employees consider cost budgets the upper limit and tend to use up cost budgets regardless of the need.	5	6	3.1%	2	11.8%
	4	37	19.4%	4	23.5%
	3	60	31.4%	2	11.8%
	2	74	38.7%	8	47.1%
	1	14	7.3%	1	5.9%
	AVG	2.723		2.882	
3 Budgeting systems do not deal with drastic changes in the business environment.	5	4	2.1%	1	5.9%
	4	36	18.8%	2	11.8%
	3	65	33.9%	10	58.8%
	2	80	41.7%	4	23.5%
	1	7	3.6%	0	0.0%
	AVG	2.740		3.000	
4 Managers negotiate lower targets than they expected.	5	4	2.1%	1	5.9%
	4	41	21.4%	5	29.4%
	3	53	27.6%	4	23.5%
	2	78	40.6%	6	35.3%
	1	16	8.3%	1	5.9%
	AVG	2.682		2.941	
5 Forecasts focus on the end of the fiscal year. Thus managers tend to engage in short-sighted behaviors.	5	4	2.1%	3	17.6%
	4	82	42.7%	7	41.2%
	3	50	26.0%	4	23.5%
	2	51	26.6%	3	17.6%
	1	5	2.6%	0	0%
	AVG	3.151		2.400	

5. Are you satisfied with your budgeting system?

There is a difference in the general situation concerning budgeting systems or alternative systems between FSCs and MCs. More FSCs answer that they are not fully satisfied with their budgeting system but that it is acceptable. They

Table 4.4 Are you satisfied with your budgeting system?

	FSCs		*MCs*	
1 Yes. We are fully satisfied with our system.	8	4.2%	0	0.0%
2 Not fully satisfied with our system but it is acceptable because we have devised effective means for our system	113	59.2%	7	41.2%
3 Not fully satisfied. We have no alternative but to use our system.	50	26.2%	8	47.1%
4 We are reforming our system to make it satisfactory.	20	10.5%	2	11.8%
	191		17	

Table 4.5 Time for budget preparation

	FSCs		*MCs*	
Less than one week	1	0.5%	0	0.0%
From one to two weeks	3	1.6%	1	6.3%
About one month	21	11.1%	3	18.8%
About one-and-a-half months	25	13.2%	3	18.8%
About two months	47	24.9%	5	31.3%
About three months	57	30.2%	4	25.0%
More than three months	35	18.5%	0	0.0%
	189		16	

seem to make their budgeting system better with various devices. On the other hand, MCs answer that because they are not fully satisfied with their budgeting system but they have no alternative, they use their budgeting system. In other words, budgeting systems are positively acceptable to FSCs and are passively acceptable to MCs.

6. Time for budget drafting

The purpose of this question is to evaluate the contention that the long time required for budget drafting causes high costs, and a change in the assumption of forecasts deprives a budget of its usefulness (see Table 4.5). The mode is about three months in FSCs, and it is about two months in MCs. In total, the time for budget drafting in MCs is shorter, which is clear in 1 in Table 4.3. According to the survey based on interviews, some companies make efforts to shorten time for budget drafting; others think that they need enough time for it in order to coordinate many divisions in-house and align division objectives with the company's overall goal.

However, the longer the time taken for budget drafting, the more obsolete the forecast information as the base of drafting. This can be avoided by re-planning budgets with forecast information.

7. Predictability

The purpose of this question is to evaluate predictability of budget drafting based on the previous survey. The easier the prediction, the higher the reliability of drafted budgets. Conversely, the more difficult the prediction, the more difficult the setting of an objective. Response values of 3 and over (neutral, easy to predict, and very easy to predict) show that prediction is easier, and values of under 3 show that it is more difficult.

Notice that values for both FSCs and MCs are under 3 in 1, 2, 4, 5, 6 in Table 4.6. More or less the difficulty of predicting became clear. Interestingly, for all the items except 2 revenues, the predictability values of MCs are higher than those of FSCs. It means that prediction in MCs is more difficult. The reasons

Table 4.6 Predictability (5: very easy to predict, 4: easy to predict, 3: neutral, 2: difficult, 1: very difficult)

		FSCs		*MCs*	
1 Key competitors' actions	5	0	0.0%	1	5.9%
	4	20	10.5%	2	11.8%
	3	91	47.6%	6	35.3%
	2	67	35.1%	8	47.1%
	1	13	6.8%	0	0.0%
	AVG	2.618		2.765	
2. Revenues	5	0	0.0%	0	0.0%
	4	37	19.4%	5	29.4%
	3	102	53.4%	5	29.4%
	2	47	24.6%	6	35.3%
	1	5	2.6%	1	5.9%
	AVG	2.895		2.824	
3. Costs	5	2	1.0%	0	0.0%
	4	83	43.5%	11	64.7%
	3	73	38.2%	6	35.3%
	2	29	15.2%	0	0.0%
	1	4	2.1%	0	0.0%
	AVG	3.262		3.647	

		FSCs		*MCs*	
4 Customer preferences and tastes	5	0	0.0%	1	5.9%
	4	25	13.2%	4	23.5%
	3	88	46.3%	9	52.9%
	2	68	35.8%	3	17.6%
	1	9	4.7%	0	0.0%
	AVG	2.679		2.941	
5 Technical innovation influencing new products	5	1	0.5%	0	0.0%
	4	18	9.6%	3	17.6%
	3	93	49.5%	10	58.8%
	2	62	33.0%	1	5.9%
	1	14	7.4%	3	17.6%
	AVG	2.628		2.765	
6 Prices of input materials purchased from suppliers	5	0	0.0%	1	6.3%
	4	16	8.4%	2	12.5%
	3	77	40.5%	8	50.0%
	2	81	42.6%	5	31.3%
	1	15	7.9%	0	0.0%
	AVG	2.484		2.938	

Questions are adapted from (Libby and Lindsay, 2010, p. 70)

are considered as follows: there are relatively many new companies in MCs, they do not have an accumulation of sufficient predicting skills, there is a considerable change in the market, and due to this, participants' behaviors are difficult to read.

8. Frequency of revenue forecasts

As shown in Table 4.6, many FSCs answer that predictability of revenues is "Neutral." In order to keep budgeting effective in such a situation, it is necessary to repeatedly predict revenues (Bogsnes, 2009; Hope and Fraser, 2005). By doing this, we can recognize the gap between prediction and budgets and targets, and take action appropriately.

Many FSCs did not select the following eleven options listed in Table 4.7, instead choosing the 12th one, "others." Moreover, many companies choose more than two ways. This means that they predict revenues with various frequencies from different points of view.

The remarkable answers are 11 at the end of the first half year, forecasting the year-end revenues and 2 monthly forecasting of the next month revenues in FSCs. Although a forecast made to review budgets on a half-year basis (11) has often been discussed, it was confirmed that many companies have made this forecast.

Table 4.7 Frequency of a revenue forecast (Multiple responses)

		FSCs		MCs	
1	No forecasting revenues	7	3.7%	0	0.0%
2	Monthly forecasting of next month revenues	77	40.3%	4	23.5%
3	Monthly forecasting of next two-month revenues	36	18.8%	3	17.6%
4	Monthly forecasting of next three-month revenues	46	24.1%	1	5.9%
5	Monthly forecasting of next quarter revenues	43	22.5%	4	23.5%
6	Quarterly forecasting of next quarter revenues	33	17.3%	0	0.0%
7	Quarterly forecasting of next two-quarter revenues. Managers forecast next fiscal year revenues.	11	5.8%	0	0.0%
8	Quarterly forecasting of next two-quarter revenues. Managers do not forecast next fiscal year revenues.	25	13.1%	4	23.5%
9	Quarterly forecasting of next four-quarter revenues. Managers forecast next fiscal year revenues.	4	2.1%	1	5.9%
10	Quarterly forecasting of next four-quarter revenues. Managers do not forecast next fiscal year revenues.	35	18.3%	1	5.9%
11	At the end of the first half year, forecasting year-end revenues	97	50.8%	6	35.3%
12	Others	47	24.6%	0	0.0%
		191		16	

On the other hand, a monthly forecast of month-end revenues (2) places more weight on considering how action should be added to achieve budgets by measuring the gap between budgets and forecasts, rather than reviewing budgets. This forecast is essential to the achievement of current-month budgets.

In BBM, a rolling forecast is an important tool. It continuously makes a forecast of the next 12-month revenues on a monthly basis, or the next four-quarter or the next five-quarter revenues on a quarterly basis. In principle the rolling forecast always makes a forecast a certain period ahead across fiscal years. Indeed, meeting the current-year budgets is a top priority, but this method is surely necessary in order that it will become customary to look a little ahead and cope with possible changes. However, there are few companies doing this, and there are many companies forecasting year-end revenues.

Other answers to this question are as follows:

- Weekly forecasting next month, next quarter, year-end revenues
- Weekly forecasting next month revenues
- Monthly forecasting year-end revenues (8)
- Monthly forecasting every month revenues within fiscal year (8)
- Monthly forecasting every quarter revenues within fiscal year (3)
- Monthly forecasting second quarter and year-end revenues
- Monthly forecasting next six-month revenues (4)

- Monthly forecasting next 12-month revenues
- Monthly forecasting year-end revenues after third quarter
- Quarterly forecasting this quarter and the next quarter revenues
- Quarterly forecasting year-end revenues (6)

Note there are only a few companies making a very distinctive rolling forecast differently from the strategies described here.

We will now examine the reliability of forecasts. Generally speaking, the longer the forecast period, the lower the reliability of forecasts. The results of the survey show this. Many FSCs and MCs give affirmative answers to the question about the reliability of revenue forecasts within one month. As shown in Table 4.8, the average response values of FSCs and MCs are 4.058 and 4.235,

Table 4.8 Reliability of a revenue forecast (5: strongly agree, 4: agree, 3: neutral, 2: disagree, 1: strongly disagree)

		FSCs		*MCs*	
1 A revenue forecast within one month is highly reliable.	5	52	27.4%	8	47.1%
	4	106	55.8%	6	35.3%
	3	23	12.1%	2	11.8%
	2	9	4.7%	1	5.9%
	1	0	0.0%	0	0.0%
	AVG	4.058		4.235	
2 A revenue forecast within one quarter is highly reliable.	5	9	4.7%	0	0.0%
	4	89	46.4%	6	35.3%
	3	70	36.5%	9	52.9%
	2	24	12.5%	1	5.9%
	1	0	0.0%	1	5.9%
	AVG	3.432		3.176	
3 A revenue forecast within a half year is highly reliable.	5	3	1.6%	0	0.0%
	4	37	19.4%	1	5.9%
	3	92	48.2%	11	64.7%
	2	55	28.8%	4	23.5%
	1	4	2.1%	1	5.9%
	AVG	2.895		2.706	
4 A revenue forecast within a year is highly reliable.	5	1	0.5%	0	0.0%
	4	25	13.1%	1	5.9%
	3	77	40.3%	8	47.1%
	2	76	39.8%	5	29.4%
	1	12	6.3%	3	17.6%
	AVG	2.618		2.412	

respectively. However, as the forecast period becomes longer (e.g., within a quarter, a half year, and a year), the reliability becomes lower.

How should we interpret this? Some people will think that because a long-term forecast is useless, it is unnecessary. However, even though it lacks reliability, it is vital to broadly forecast future revenues and make an effort to fill the gaps between forecasts and targets. Even though a forecast cannot be made in detail, it is important for an organization to share information about what will happen.

9. Action taken when forecasted revenues are lower than budgeted revenues

Next, I examined what action was taken when revenues were forecasted. Tables 4.9 and 4.10 show the results in cases where forecasted revenues are

Table 4.9 Revising revenue targets downward or not? (Multiple responses)

	FSCs		*MCs*	
1 Encouraging managers to achieve their initial targets. The targets are not revised downward unless in extreme circumstances.	100	52.6%	8	50.0%
2 Revising initial targets downward. Revision is reviewed at the end of every month.	23	12.1%	2	12.5%
3 Revising initial targets downward. Revision is reviewed at the end of every quarter.	51	26.8%	4	25.0%
4 Revising initial targets downward. Revision is reviewed at the end of every half year.	39	20.5%	3	18.8%
	190		16	

Table 4.10 Revising cost targets downward or not? (Multiple responses)

	FSCs		*MCs*	
1 Budgeted costs are not revised downward even though forecasted revenues are lower than budgeted revenues.	61	33.0%	4	23.5%
2 Budgeted costs are revised downward when forecasted revenues are lower than budgeted revenues. Revision is reviewed at the end of every month.	44	23.8%	4	23.5%
3 Budgeted costs are revised downward when forecasted revenues are lower than budgeted revenues. Revision is reviewed at the end of every quarter.	48	25.9%	3	17.6%
4 Budgeted costs are revised downward when forecasted revenues are lower than budgeted revenues. Revision is reviewed at the end of every half year.	47	25.4%	5	29.4%
	185		17	

lower than budgeted revenues (targets). Such a situation usually happens because budgeted revenues should be set as a stretched target. I asked whether revenues and cost targets were revised under this situation.

It is a stereotyped way of thinking in Japan that even though forecasted revenues are low, companies keep budgeted revenues as they are, without making a revision and an effort to attain them. According to the results of an interview survey, many companies keep their initial targets as they are because if the targets are revised downward by low forecasted revenues, no one seriously makes an effort to meet the targets. Even so, approximately 60 percent of the companies answer that they revise their initial targets downward. Budgeted revenues are quite flexible.

Incidentally, although the targets are not officially revised downward, in fact downward-revised targets termed "Chakuchi-ten" are used in many companies. It means that there are two targets: official targets and Chakuchi-ten as a target to be surely achieved.

Budgeted costs are often revised downward when forecasted revenues are low. Naturally, a way of thinking to make profits seems to establish itself.

10. Action taken when forecasted revenues are higher than budgeted revenues

In contrast, Table 4.11 and 4.12 show situations that occur when forecasted revenues are higher than budgeted revenues. In this case, the percentages of both FSCs and MCs answering that they do not revise their initial targets upward are the largest, but their percentages are a little smaller than those of FSCs and MCs not revising downward in Table 4.9.

Over 50 percent of FSCs answer that as a rule they do not approve of adding budgeted costs even though forecasted revenues are higher than budgeted revenues, and this result is in clear contrast to result 1 in Table 4.10. However, companies considering an upward revision as well as a downward revision are in the majority.

Table 4.11 Revising revenue targets upward or not? (Multiple responses)

	FSCs		*MCs*	
1 Targets are not revised upward unless in extreme circumstances.	87	46.0%	6	40.0%
2 Revising initial targets upward. Revision is reviewed at the end of every month.	26	13.8%	2	13.3%
3 Revising initial targets upward. Revision is reviewed at the end of every quarter.	54	28.6%	4	26.7%
4 Revising initial targets upward. Revision is reviewed at the end of every half year.	38	20.1%	3	20.0%
	189		15	

Table 4.12 Revising cost targets upward or not? (Multiple responses)

	FSCs		*MCs*	
1 Budgeted costs are not revised upward even though forecasted revenues are higher than budgeted revenues.	100	54.1%	6	37.5%
2 Budgeted costs are revised upward when forecasted revenues are higher than budgeted revenues. Revision is reviewed at the end of every month.	29	15.7%	2	12.5%
3 Budgeted costs are revised upward when forecasted revenues are higher than budgeted revenues. Revision is reviewed at the end of every quarter.	30	16.2%	3	18.8%
4 Budgeted costs are revised upward when forecasted revenues are higher than budgeted revenues. Revision is reviewed at the end of every half year.	33	17.8%	4	25.0%
	185		17	

Table 4.13 Target setting in divisions

	FSCs		*MCs*	
1 Divisions commit themselves to attain profit targets. A head office does not check revenue targets nor budgeted costs.	3	1.6%	0	0.0%
2 Divisions commit themselves to attain profit targets. A head office receives the information of revenue targets and budgeted costs but does not intervene.	47	25.4%	3	21.4%
3 Divisions commit themselves to attain not only profit targets but also revenue targets and budgeted costs.	135	73.0%	11	78.6%
	185		14	

11. Target setting in divisions

I asked whether the targets in divisions and departments (profit centers) are profits or are set on revenues and costs. A profit center is responsible for profits, and because in theory its manager takes responsibility for profits, he/she ought to have the discretion on revenues and costs. However, in fact a head office may intervene in the divisions' and departments' control of revenues and costs.

As a result, the sum of 1 and 2 (Divisions commit themselves to attain profit targets) in Table 4.13 is 27 percent in FSCs and 21.4 percent in MCs. And in over 70 percent of both FSCs and MCs, divisions commit themselves to attain revenue targets and budgeted costs in order to achieve profit targets.

12. Attempt to make targets in divisions stretch

It is pointed out that one of the problems with budgets is that easy-to-achieve targets tend to be set (Table 4.3, 4). Many companies are working on overcoming this problem. It has conventionally been overcome by negotiations between a head office and divisions and departments to set high targets desired through a company. That is definitely clarified in Table 4.14, 2.

There are some interesting results. For example, in Table 4.14, 3, we can see that approximately 20 percent of both FSCs and MCs disclose a league table of targets and encourage competition in divisions and departments for high targets. This is one type of social control, and means disclosing various information and controlling the operation with the eyes of all the people. Some companies make a table of ranking called a league table. Generally in Japan, unlike in Europe and the United States, the rankings of this league table are not closely tied to rewards. However, few managers in the low ranking remain calm, and this league table is reported to work effectively (Hope and Fraser, 2005).

There are also some companies measuring the setting of targets itself. 14.8 percent of FSCs and 20 percent of MCs measure the stretch of targets (4). Although it is difficult to clarify what the criteria for judging the stretch of targets are, 4 shows not only whether managers attain their targets, but also the level of difficulty of the targets they try to meet.

Moreover, there are some companies focusing attention on the importance of corporate culture. As shown in 6, approximately 20 percent of both FSCs

Table 4.14 Attempt to make targets in divisions stretch (multiple responses)

	FSCs		*MCs*	
1 Corporate directs division managers to set stretch targets.	57	30.2%	2	13.3%
2 Corporate negotiates with division managers to set stretch targets.	132	69.8%	8	53.3%
3 Corporate makes and discloses a league table of all division targets and brings divisions into competition for high targets.	36	19.0%	3	20.0%
4 Corporate measures not only the degree of attainment but also the degree of stretch.	28	14.8%	3	20.0%
5 Corporate directs division managers to set higher targets than the previous fiscal year performance.	38	20.1%	3	20.0%
6 In-house education is provided. Employees are educated to do their best at all times. Corporate strives to have a corporate culture in which employees try to do their best.	33	17.5%	3	20.0%
7 Others	4	2.1%	0	0.0%
	189		15	

and MCs provide in-house education for their employees so that they can do their best work, and aim to cultivate a healthy corporate culture. These points form a background to make employees move appropriately by using budgeting as a tool, and are a major focus of recent studies of management control.

13. Performance measurement items of profit centers

Table 4.15 shows the results of the question, "What do you use as performance measurement items of profit centers?" While the degree of the attainment of profit targets is most used in FSCs, the degree of the attainment of revenue targets is most used in MCs. The latter reflects characteristics of the Mothers market, largely composed of growth companies. Placing a special emphasis on the degree of the attainment of revenue targets is characteristic of Japanese companies. It is certain that a quantitative expansion was directly linked to corporate profit increases during the period of rapid economic growth. However, although after the collapse of the bubble economy a quantitative expansion came to an end, it still tends to be pursued. For matured industries as well as for companies that still have more room for growth like MCs, it may be risky to pursue such a quantitative expansion. In that sense, it is considered right that FSCs tend to put an emphasis on profit targets. According to various surveys, Japanese companies tend to place more importance on the amount of profit than the rate of return. Besides this tendency, that few Japanese companies use ROE is also criticized by foreign investors. The use of ROI and ROE should be advanced in order to make awareness of investment efficiency clear for middle managers such as division managers.

Not only the measures of results but the measures of behavior – for example, the appropriateness of action plans and behavioral evaluation – are used. This

Table 4.15 Performance measurement items of profit centers (multiple responses)

	FSCs		*MCs*	
1 Degree of attainment of targets; amount of profits and/or profit margin on sales	154	84.2%	11	68.8%
2 Degree of attainment of targets; amount of revenues	123	67.2%	14	87.5%
3 Degree of attainment of targets; amount of costs	44	24.0%	1	6.3%
4 Degree of stretch on targets	19	10.4%	1	6.3%
5 Appropriateness of action plans to attain targets	56	30.6%	4	25.0%
6 Behavioral evaluation except financial results	65	35.5%	6	37.5%
	183		16	

is extremely necessary for division and department managers, and awareness of ROI and ROE is important. However, it is often impossible for divisions to control capital costs and the amount of investment. Accordingly, measures to increase ROE, improving sales, reducing costs, increasing inventory turnover, and improving receivable turnover are deployed into the normal operation. As to these approaches (especially improving sales and reducing costs), specific action plans are necessary, and it becomes extremely important to evaluate whether the plans are appropriately made and properly executed.

14. Performance measurement items of profit-center managers

Although Section 13 showed the survey results of performance measurement items of profit centers, this section describes which performance measurement items are most important to profit-center "managers." It is only for the items focused on the degree of attainment of profit targets in FSCs and

Table 4.16 Performance measurement items of profit-center managers (multiple responses; 5: very important, 4: important, 3: neutral, 2: not very important, 1: not important)

		FSCs		*MCs*	
1 Degree of attainment of targets; amount of profits and/or profit margin on sales	5	98	53.0%	6	42.9%
	4	68	36.8%	6	42.9%
	3	16	8.6%	1	7.1%
	2	2	1.1%	0	0.0%
	1	1	0.5%	1	7.1%
	AVG	4.405		4.143	
2 Degree of attainment of targets; amount of revenues	5	50	27.0%	6	40.0%
	4	85	45.9%	9	60.0%
	3	34	18.4%	0	0.0%
	2	13	7.0%	0	0.0%
	1	3	1.3%	0	0.0%
	AVG	3.897		4.400	
3 Degree of attainment of targets; amount of costs	5	14	7.7%	0	0.0%
	4	58	31.7%	3	25.0%
	3	72	39.3%	6	50.0%
	2	28	15.3%	2	16.7%
	1	11	6.0%	1	8.3%
	AVG	3.197		2.917	

(*Continued*)

Table 4.16 (Continued)

		FSCs		*MCs*	
4 Degree of stretch on targets	5	4	2.2%	0	0.0%
	4	49	27.2%	3	23.1%
	3	85	47.2%	7	53.8%
	2	34	18.9%	2	15.4%
	1	8	4.4%	1	7.7%
	AVG	3.039		2.923	
5 Appropriateness of action plans to attain targets	5	12	6.6%	0	0.0%
	4	92	50.8%	8	53.3%
	3	54	29.8%	6	40.0%
	2	14	7.7%	0	0.0%
	1	9	5.0%	1	6.7%
	AVG	3.464		3.400	
6 Behavioral evaluation except financial results (for example, the multi-aspect performance measurement by using Balanced Scorecard)	5	9	2.8%	0	0.0%
	4	67	10.2%	5	35.7%
	3	78	44.1%	7	50.0%
	2	18	10.2%	1	7.1%
	1	5	2.8%	1	7.1%
	AVG	3.322		3.143	

the degree of attainment of profit targets and revenue targets in MCs that the average response value is over four points. Apparently this result in MCs derives from the fact that an emergent market makes much of the expansion of scale.

Concerning the appropriateness of action plans, the average value is over 3.4 points in both FSCs and MCs. This relatively high value demonstrates that a process as well as a result becomes an object of performance measurement.

15. Impact of the degree of budget attainment by managers on their bonuses

This question relates to how closely profit-center managers' bonuses are tied to the degree of budget attainment. Although the merits and demerits of pay per performance systems are frequently discussed, generally in Japan a bonus is seldom tied to individual performance, and it is said that company-wide performance is the major factor in determining the amount of a bonus.

The survey results show that in both FSCs and MCs the response that the amount of a bonus depends on the degree of attainment of company-wide financial

Table 4.17 Impact of the degree of budget attainment of managers on their bonuses

	FSCs		*MCs*	
1 No or little impact of the degree of budget attainment of managers on their bonuses. The amount of a bonus mainly depends on the degree of company-wide budget attainment.	31	17.1%	5	31.3%
2 There are two factors that impact on the amount of a bonus: the degree of company-wide budget attainment and the degree of division budget attainment.	87	48.1%	6	37.5%
3 There are three factors that impact on the amount of a bonus: the degree of company-wide budget attainment, the degree of division budget attainment, and the degree of attainment of non-financial KPI targets of managers.	19	10.5%	2	12.5%
4 There are four factors that impact on the amount of a bonus: the degree of company-wide budget attainment, the degree of division budget attainment, the degree of attainment of non-financial KPI targets of managers, and their behavioral evaluation.	44	24.3%	3	18.8%
	181		16	

targets and profit-center financial targets is the mode (see Table 4.7). However, although 31.3 percent of MCs respond that the degree of attainment of company-wide financial targets is a factor in determining the amount of a bonus, there are also relatively many companies responding that the degree of attainment of non-financial KPI targets and the evaluation of managers' behavior are factors. A further survey needs to be conducted as to whether a bonus is used as an incentive.

16. Results

These survey results reveal that many companies make efforts to improve their budgeting systems in terms of forecasting, reviewing, and re-planning budgets. The results show that Japanese companies execute the many features of BBM detailed in Chapter 10; that is, the use of forecasts in implementing plans. As Lorain (2010) said, a rolling forecast serves as a good complement to budgeting under uncertain management conditions. That is because companies consider early what to do in order to achieve their goals by forecasting the future.

The longer the forecasting period, the less reliance is put on forecasting. Therefore, forecasting by the month or the quarter is meaningful. Approximately 80 percent of Japanese companies forecast revenues of the next month, the next two months, or the next three months on a monthly basis, and cope with changes in the future quickly.

However, forecasts in most Japanese companies are not made in a pure form of a rolling forecast because the forecasts do not include forecasts of the next year. This clearly causes problems that the response to the next fiscal year is slow and short-sighted activities are induced. Table 4.7 reveals that there are only a few companies making a pure rolling forecast. Demonstrating the effectiveness of rolling forecasts in these companies will increase the number of companies adopting rolling forecasts.

A forecast is just a forecast. Measuring the gap between a forecast and a target must lead to concrete actions to fill the gap. When forecasted revenues are lower than budgeted revenue targets, over half of the companies surveyed change initial revenue targets and over two-thirds of companies make a downward revision of initial cost budgets. When forecasted revenues are higher than budgeted revenue targets, over two-thirds of companies make an upward revision of initial revenue targets but half of them do not change cost budgets. This means that companies change both revenue budgets and cost budgets to cope with changing environments; in other words, companies change their plans. Re-planning revenues and costs becomes effective measures to overcome the inability to cope with environments flexibly, which is one of the biggest problems with budgeting systems. Because Japanese companies have already adopted those measures, they will not probably regard 2, and 3, and 4 in Table 4.3 as significant problems. However, because forecasts at the end of the fiscal year are made, short-sighted behavior remains problematic.

On the other hand, setting stretch targets depends on only traditional methods (1 and 2 in Table 4.14), and it is not an object of evaluation of division managers. Concerning whether division managers set stretch targets voluntarily and how such behavior is induced, a further survey is needed.

The surveys described in this chapter focus mainly on cybernetic controls and do not deal with things leading employees to right behavior, such as a mission, behavioral precepts, and a corporate culture. Especially how a corporate culture has an influence on budgeting systems is a subject to be identified in the future.

(This chapter is based on and adopted from Shimizu (2016) with permission of Waseda Shogaku Doukoukai. This research is a part of the outcome of research performed by the fund from the Melco Foundation.)

References

Bogsnes, B. (2009) *Implementing Beyond Budgeting: Unlocking the Performance Potential*, Hoboken, NJ: John Wiley & Sons.

Hope, J. and R. Fraser (2005) *Beyond Budgeting: How Managers Can Break Free from the Annual Performance Trap*, Boston, MA: Harvard Business School Press.

Libby, T. and R.M. Lindsay (2010) Beyond budgeting or budgeting reconsidered? A survey of North-American budgeting practice, *Management Accounting Research*, 21(1), 56–75.

Lorain, MA. (2010) Should rolling forecasts replace budgets in uncertain environments?, in Epstain, M.J., J.F. Manzoni, and A. Davila (eds.) *Performance Measurement and Management Control: Innovative Concepts and Practices*, Bingley, UK: Emerald Group Publishing Limited, pp. 177–208.

Shimizu, T. (2013) *Performance Management to Implement Strategy*, Tokyo, Japan: Chuokeizai-sha Inc. Written in Japanese.

Shimizu, T. (2016) A survey of the improvement of budgeting systems in Japanese companies, *Waseda Business Review* (Waseda University), 446, pp. 103–130. Written in Japanese.

Yokota, E., A. Takada, T. Senoo, and S. Kaneko (2012) A survey of management control systems and behavior of managers in Japanese companies, *Mita Business Review* (Keio University), 55(4), 93–106.

5 Management in decentralized Japanese companies

Key learning points

- Many large companies employ decentralized organizations. Why?
- What are the merits and demerits of decentralization?
- There are two systems in decentralized organization: a functional system and a division system.
- What are the features of a division system from the perspectives of internal interest or internal dividends, allocation of corporate costs, and evaluation of managers in Japan?

1. What is decentralization? Decentralized and centralized organizations

Management in organizations can be either centralized or decentralized. When an organization is small in scale and top management can manage all organizational behavior, a centralized form – with top management consisting of one person or a few persons – is sufficient to make all plans in the organization and control them. In traditional companies, top management has the power of making all decisions. That is because only top management is considered to have skills and knowledge to make decisions. However, when an organization is big in scale, it is difficult for top management to obtain all information and make the proper decisions for environmental adaptation. Especially when a company is diversified and enters other business domains, managers need to acquire new knowledge about markets, customers, and technologies. The organization is therefore decentralized.

2. Features of decentralization

Decentralized organizations are divided into two types: divisional organizations and functional organizations. The former is more decentralized than the latter.

Decentralization is the freedom for managers at lower levels of the organization to make decisions (Horngren et al., 2012, p. 777). In decentralized organizations, authority is transferred from one hierarchy to a lower one. This is termed *empowerment*, which is one of the biggest features of decentralization.

Chandler (1962) explained decentralization by linking it with diversification. As the degree of diversification increases, an organization changes from a centralized functional organization to a decentralized divisional one. A famous example of early decentralized companies in Japan is Panasonic. Konosuke Matsushita produced plugs in 1927. In addition, he started his new business making heating wires. Because he was unfamiliar with this product, he left the business up to persons with more experience. This management by entrustment was the beginning of a division system in Panasonic. After that, it started management via a full-dress division system consisting of three divisions in 1933. Each division had factories and sales bases, and each division was responsible for all business including R&D, manufacturing, and sales.[1]

The characteristics of decentralization are

1 To make decisions in a timely manner. Decision making takes a long time in a large centralized organization due to multilayered hierarchy.
2 To make decisions properly. Division managers know their business and business environments much better than top management.

Under turbulent circumstances, it is critical for companies to take quick and appropriate measures against changing management environments. The changing environments, such as customers' preference, technologies, and resource prices, are recognized by front-line employees. To deal with these conditions timely and appropriately, division managers should be empowered to make decisions about their operations. In centralized organizations, it takes a long time for top management to receive a report on what is happening on the front line and to give orders to front-line employees.

3. Merits and demerits of decentralization

Decentralization has merits and demerits. The merits are

1 Division managers make quick decisions.
2 Division managers with a wide range of autonomy for decision making have higher motivation.
3 Division managers learn management skills.
4 Division managers focus on management of divisions' operations. This enables top management to focus on company-wide strategy.

As mentioned before, in rapidly changing environments, it is necessary to recognize these changes quickly and cope with them as soon as possible. Consequently, authorization for divisions' operations needs to be given to division managers.

Empowering division managers to manage their divisions gives managers a high degree of autonomy to make decisions in their divisions. The more autonomy they have, the more motivation they have.

Division managers can experience top management's work by operating their own divisions because they must make plans, form action plans to implement the plans, coordinate functions, measure performance, and evaluate their subordinates. All of these train the next generation's skills as top management.

Also, by entrusting divisions' operations to division managers, top management can concentrate on corporate strategy planning and its implementation.

In contrast, the demerits of decentralization are

1 Division managers sometimes make suboptimal decisions.
2 Decentralized organizations are more costly than centralized ones.
3 Different divisions sometimes manufacture similar products.

First, division managers manage their divisions' operations and make an effort to achieve targets desired by top management. When a division is set as a profit center or an investment center, some division managers may attempt to maximize their own division's profits, sacrificing other divisions' and company-wide profits. This case becomes conspicuous when divisions interact closely (e.g., vertical diversification or functional systems).

Second, while centralized organizations set management functions in only one place, in decentralized organizations, each division has a part of management functions (e.g., an accounting department and an HR department), and this is redundant.

Finally, because each division might manufacture and sell similar products, this may lead to cannibalization. Yamazaki Baking Co., Ltd., is a large bakery in Japan, and its consolidated sales in 2015 were 1,027 billion yen. The Lunch-Pack series is representative of products in Yamazaki. It is a type of sandwich and a popular product. On Yamazaki's website (http://www.yamazakipan.co.jp/lunch-p/lineup-gallery/backnumber.php), as of December 2015 about 50 kinds of products including bread products, such as chocolate cream, whipped cream, and fruit jam, and prepared food products, such as curry, croquette, and teriyaki chicken, are listed.

Yamazaki has deployed about 25 factories throughout the country, and each of them works on the product development of the Lunch-Pack. Consequently, they can develop products reflecting customer tastes in the region and local special products. This is the main reason why the Lunch-Pack is widely popular.

On the other hand, because each factory works on its own product development, it often develops products similar to other factories' products. For example, two kinds of curry products, three kinds of strawberry flavor products, and three kinds of Japanese chow mein products are sold. The curry products have very similar names: cheese and curry, and curry and cheese cream. On a list of products produced and sold in the past, consumers were sometimes confused by some products.

This example explains the merits and demerits of decentralization. Factories in different regions grasp local needs, and develop, produce, and sell local products. A head office cannot do that. At the same time, the fact that different factories often develop similar products causes redundancy.

4. Decentralization and responsibility centers

A responsibility center is an important factor in responsibility accounting. In responsibility accounting, a subunit of an organization focuses on specific activities to accomplish. A subunit is responsible for only these activities.

The concept of "controllable or uncontrollable" is critical in responsibility accounting. Subunit managers take responsibility for only the results of their controllable activities because burdening managers with responsibility for their uncontrollable tasks damages their motivation.

Responsibility centers are divided into a variety of groups according to the range of responsibility:

1 Cost center: In a cost center, managers are responsible for only costs in their subunits. For example, a manufacturing division manager is responsible for manufacturing costs but not responsible for sales costs. The departments that do not directly earn revenues, such as administration, storage, and R&D departments, are also included in the cost center.
2 Revenue center: In a revenue center, managers are responsible for revenues. Sales divisions can be included in the revenue center.
3 Profit center: In a profit center, managers are responsible for profits. It means that they are also responsible for revenues and costs because profits are the difference between revenues and costs. Managers have all the authority to make profits. They make many plans to manufacture products and sell them. They also research the market, develop products, and promote products.
4 Investment center: In an investment center, managers are responsible for the relationship between profits of their subunits and an investment amount in subunits. It means that they are responsible for revenues, costs, and investments. Managers can decide to invest in their subunits. Managers are required to earn the biggest profits by using their assets as efficiently as possible. Managers in the investment center have the widest range of authority and responsibility of the four centers.

5. A functional system and a division system

Decentralization has two systems: a functional system and a division system. The division system is more decentralized than the functional system. This section describes these two systems in detail.

Functional system

A large-scale organization may be decentralized by function. The functions include development, production, sales, marketing, accounting, HR, and so on. Each function becomes an independent organization and has a manager.

Look at Figure 5.1. A central office formulates a strategy and communicates it to each function. Because each division is set by function, a division vice-president (VP) has responsibility for each function. Division VPs often have

Figure 5.1 A functional system

limited accountability. For example, a VP of manufacturing is responsible for manufacturing costs. And a VP of marketing is responsible for sales and sometimes sales costs. When a VP of manufacturing is responsible for manufacturing costs, the manufacturing division is the "cost center." When a VP of marketing is responsible for only revenues, the marketing division is the "revenue center," but when a VP of marketing is responsible for profits, revenues minus costs, it is the "profit center."

Generally, each division in a functional system is set as a cost center or a revenue center. However, these divisions can be set as profit centers or investment centers. In this case, a transfer pricing system is required. Transfer price is an internal price that is set when products or services are transferred from a division or a department to other divisions or departments. The transfer pricing system sometimes causes troubles. I will take up these problems in Chapter 9.

In Japan many companies adopt a functional system. A representative example is Toyota Motor Corporation.

Division system

Next, let us look at a division system. In the division system each division has all the functions including manufacturing and sales necessary for management as shown in Figure 5.2. These divisions are set by product or area. A product division has all the functions to develop, manufacture, sell specific products, and manage its business. A regional division has all the functions to develop, manufacture, sell products in a certain area, and manage its business. Therefore, divisions in the division system ought to be the profit center. And when a division VP has the authority to invest in his/her businesses, the division is the investment center and the VP takes responsibility for revenues, costs, and investments.

VPs in the functional system have only limited authority. They are often interested in only their functional performance. Thus to make a decision to attain the best performance for a company, top management in the central office

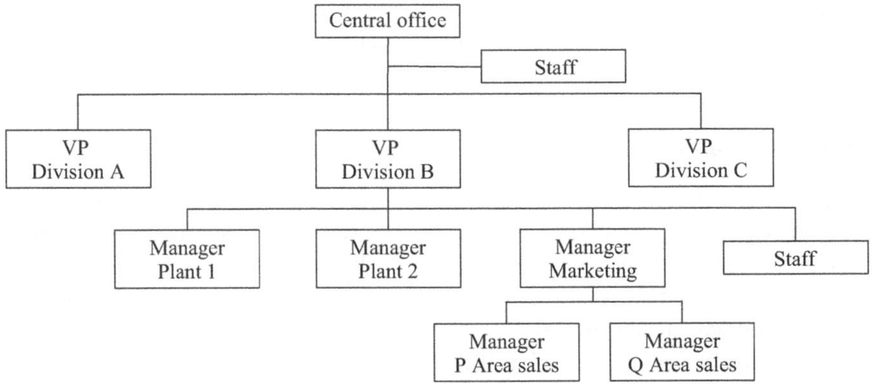

Figure 5.2 A division system

ought to intervene between the two divisions, such as a manufacturing division and a marketing division.

On the other hand, VPs in the division system have the broader authority to research and develop, manufacture, and sell products. They must coordinate these functions in their divisions to maximize profits. Companies with unrelated diversification, such as General Electric, do not need to coordinate divisions because they are basically independent. However, companies with related diversification, such as paper manufacturing companies, need to coordinate divisions because a product of a division is transferred to another division. While transferring a product is the optimum decision for a company, it may not be the optimum decision for a division manufacturing a product, for example. In this case, the division manager may make a decision not to manufacture the product. Then a central office can intervene in this problem in order to lead a company to the optimum conditions. The problem with transfer pricing is an example of sub-optimization. This is mentioned in Chapter 9.

6. The features of a division system in Japan

The division system adopted by many Japanese companies has some different features from those of the division system developed in the United States. In many cases, divisions in Japan do not have the authority to invest. A central office has the authority and responsibility for investing in divisions, and division managers are committed to making profits by using assets that are invested by a central office. Consequently, in Japan, a division is just a profit center, not an investment center.

In the 1980s some Japanese companies adopted a real division system whose managers have broader authorities, and it is called the company system. In this system, each division was called a "company." This means that the company is an internal company. The company system is a Japanese-style division system and has at least two remarkable features: internal capital and internal interest or internal dividends. I will give a brief explanation of each feature in the following sections.

Internal capital

Each division has not only an income statement but also a balance sheet. The reason why it has a balance sheet is that division managers manage the total assets in their divisions and control ROA or ROE. To make a balance sheet of a division, all assets, liabilities, and capital must be recognized in each division. It is not difficult to assign assets and liabilities to each division. Assets occupied by a division are assigned to that division. Shared assets[2] should be allocated to divisions on some allocation bases.

On the other hand, it is more difficult to allocate capital to divisions. There are some methods for the allocation. First, company-wide net assets are allocated to each division on an allocation basis, for example at the rate of assets in a division. In this case, assets may be the sum of inventory assets and fixed assets (Kobayashi, 2009, p. 448). And the total of a division's capital is equal to company-wide net assets at the starting point of the internal capital system. Second, the deductive method is used. At the starting point of the internal capital system, each division has been assigned and allocated assets and liabilities. After this its capital is calculated as the difference between its assets and liabilities. Third, division capital can be calculated by ROE of the same type of company. In these two cases, the total of a division's capital is not equal to company-wide net assets.

Recently, ROE (return on equity) has become an important KPI for companies as one of the measures of the contribution to shareholders. By allocating net assets to divisions as division capital, a head office can encourage division managers to raise ROE, and can give them the authority to reinvest a part of profits earned by divisions. Providing this authority is useful for increasing division managers' motivation.

Internal interest or internal dividends

A division can recognize the source of its funding – that is, liabilities and capital – by having a balance sheet. Whether the source of funding is liabilities or capital, the cost of capital is incurred by raising cash. In order to make division managers well aware of the cost of capital and minimize it, it is necessary to charge the cost of capital to divisions. There are some methods for charging.

One of the methods is to charge the different cost of capital by the source of funding. When a company introduces the company system, a central office gives internal capital to each company. In this case, the company has to pay an internal dividend to the central office. When the company needs more money after getting its capital, the central office lends money to the company. Of course, the company has to pay internal interest to the central office.

Another method is to calculate the company-wide weighted average cost of capital (WACC), multiply that result by total assets in a company to figure out the amount of cost of capital, and charge it to the company. This way of thinking is identical with the idea of Economic Value Added (EVA®). This method eliminates the need for classification of the creditor into liabilities and internal capital, and therefore is relatively easy to carry out. Moreover, by adopting this method a head office enables division managers to pay more attention to the cost of capital. There is the view that the cost of capital is not useful in division management because division managers do not have the authority to determine the cost of capital and it is uncontrollable for them. Some Japanese companies accept this view, but others do not. The relationship between controllability and managers' decision and performance evaluation is described in detail later.

7. Income statements of decentralized organizations

Table 5.1 is a sample of an income statement in a division system[3] that is often used by Japanese companies.

Contribution margin is calculated by subtracting variable manufacturing costs and variable sales costs from sales. Fixed costs are divided into three groups: controllable fixed costs, uncontrollable fixed costs, and corporate costs. Controllable costs are costs for which division managers have authority, such as labor costs, some administrative costs of their divisions, and advertisement costs. These costs are paid by the decision of division managers. Thus controllable profits are appropriate to measure the performance of division managers. Uncontrollable fixed costs are costs for which division managers do not have authority,

Table 5.1 An income statement of a division (A)

	Division A	*Division B*	*Division C*	*Total*
Sales	xxx	xxx	xxx	xxx
Variable manufacturing costs	xxx	xxx	xxx	xxx
Variable sales costs	xxx	xxx	xxx	xxx
Contribution margin	xxx	xxx	xxx	xxx
Controllable fixed costs	xxx	xxx	xxx	xxx
Controllable profits	xxx	xxx	xxx	xxx
Uncontrollable fixed costs	xxx	xxx	xxx	xxx
Division profits	xxx	xxx	xxx	xxx
Corporate costs				xxx
Net income before tax				xxx

but these costs are easily traced to the division that spends them. For example, when a division manager does not have any authority to invest in equipment, depreciation of equipment in this division is an uncontrollable fixed cost. Division profits cannot be used for the evaluation of division managers but are useful for the evaluation of a division itself – that is, in determining whether or not the division deserves continuing investment.

Corporate costs are administrative costs used by a head office. They are paid for operation in the whole company and used as costs common to some divisions. In U.S. textbooks, these costs are not allocated to each division but are just subtracted from the total of division profits in each division.

8. Performance measures of divisions

To measure the performance of divisions, typical performance indicators include return on sales (ROS), return on investment (ROI), and residual income (RI).

Return on sales

Return on sales is the percentage of income to net sales (revenues) and is calculated as follows:

$$\text{ROS} = \text{Income} \div \text{Net Sales (Revenues)}$$

ROS shows the income per dollar of revenues and the profitability of revenues. To use ROS for measuring a division manager or a division itself, controllable profits or division profits are appropriate. While ROS is proper when the amount of investment in each division is not calculated, ROI is better as a performance indicator when the amount of investment is calculated.

Return on investment

ROI is the percentage of income to the total investment and is calculated as follows:

$$\text{ROI} = \text{Income} \div \text{Investment}$$

ROI shows the percentage of income earned by using company's assets and is a comprehensive performance indicator of profitability. The reason why it is "a comprehensive performance indicator" is that it includes all of the important factors in the business, including revenues, costs, and investment. To use ROI, the amount of investment in each division needs to be calculated, but each division does not need a balance sheet.

To measure the performance of a division, the amount of investment in this division and division profits should be recognized because ROI is a measure of a division's profitability.

Generally, ROI is divided into two factors: ROS and capital turnover.

$$\text{ROI} = \text{ROS} \times \text{Capital Turnover} = \frac{\textit{Net Income}}{\textit{Sales}} \times \frac{\textit{Sales}}{\textit{Investment}}$$

According to this formula, divisions or companies should increase ROS by increasing income per sales, and/or increase capital turnover by using investment efficiently to generate sales to improve their ROI.

Residual income

It is sometimes said that ROI may cause a division manager to make a sub-optimized decision. For example, if a division makes an investment of ¥10 billion and earns ¥1 billion, ROI is 10 percent. Now the manager of this division is considering the new opportunity of an investment of ¥1 billion, and the manager estimates income earned from this investment at ¥0.08 billion. In this case the manager may make a decision not to invest in this opportunity because ROI of this division comes down from 10 percent to 9.82 percent ((1+0.08) ÷ (10+1)).

However, when the required ROI is 7 percent, is this decision good for this company, but not for this division? The answer is, of course, emphatically "no." Even though ROI decreases, this manager should invest in this opportunity to increase the corporate value.

To align a division's decision with a company's optimal decision, using residual income (RI) is recommended. RI is calculated as follows:

$$\text{RI} = \text{Income} - \text{Required Rate of Return} \times \text{Investment}$$

Operating income is usually used as "income" in this formula. The required rate of return is also known as the hurdle rate – the minimum rate of return – and it is a criterion for deciding whether or not to invest in a business. Generally, the cost of capital is used as the required rate of return. This is because the cost of capital includes costs of raising funds and costs incurred inevitably by investment. There are two concepts regarding cost of capital. One is the percentage and the other is the amount. Cost of capital expressed in percentage is the weighted average of cost of capital (WACC) of liabilities and that of net assets. Cost of capital expressed in amounts is calculated by the product of cost of capital expressed in percentage and an investment amount.

Let us calculate RI by using the previous example.

Current Situation: ¥1 billion – 0.07 × ¥10 billion = ¥300 million
After Investment: ¥1.1 billion – 0.07 × ¥11 billion = ¥330 million

Using RI, this division manager makes an investment in this opportunity because this investment increases RI in this division. Consequently, it is said that RI can solve the sub-optimization problem of ROI in the explained situation.

ROI has merits and demerits. The typical merit is that ROI has all the important factors of business: revenues, costs, and investment, and therefore this is a comprehensive measure of profitability. One more merit is that we can compare some investment plans by using ROI because it is shown as percentage. The demerit is that managers may make a suboptimal decision. RI also has merits and demerits. The typical merit of RI is to avoid ROI's demerits. The typical demerit is that RI is affected by the scale of investment because it is an "amount," not a percentage.

The concept of *cost of capital* is critical to managing operations of companies. However, I think we can avoid the sub-optimization of ROI by showing cost of capital that is equal to the required return to division managers. That is to say, when top managers need to show the value of cost of capital to division managers and should tell them when ROI from new investments exceeds the cost of capital, they obtain a high appraisal.

9. Allocation of corporate costs

In Japan, many companies use different types of income statements in the division system. See Table 5.2.

The difference between Table 5.1 and 5.2 is simple. The point is whether or not corporate costs are allocated to each division. As stated before, corporate costs are uncontrollable for division managers. However, they are necessary for operating the whole company. Moreover, each division sometimes uses services from the corporate headquarters. In this case, especially the cost drivers of corporate costs are clear, and corporate costs should be allocated to divisions.

Table 5.2 An income statement of a division (B)

	Division A	*Division B*	*Division C*	*Total*
Sales	xxx	xxx	xxx	xxx
Variable manufacturing costs	xxx	xxx	xxx	xxx
Variable sales costs	xxx	xxx	xxx	xxx
Contribution margin	xxx	xxx	xxx	xxx
Controllable fixed costs	xxx	xxx	xxx	xxx
Controllable profits	xxx	xxx	xxx	xxx
Uncontrollable fixed costs	xxx	xxx	xxx	xxx
Division profits	xxx	xxx	xxx	xxx
Corporate costs	xxx	xxx	xxx	xxx
Net income before tax	xxx	xxx	xxx	xxx

Companies have three ways to account for corporate costs: to allocate all of the corporate costs to divisions, to allocate no corporate costs, and to allocate only corporate costs that have a rational cost driver. The last option is preferred for some decision purposes in the United States (Horngren et al., 2012, p. 508).

In Japan, most companies allocate corporate costs to divisions. According to one study,[4] 88.6 percent of the respondents in the non-manufacturing sector and 94.7 percent of the respondents in the manufacturing sector allocate corporate costs to divisions. Many other studies show the same results.[5]

Why do Japanese companies allocate corporate costs even though corporate costs are uncontrollable for division managers? There are some reasons for it.

First, and most importantly, allocating corporate costs reinforces a mutual check and balance. The corporate headquarters costs are always checked by divisions. Divisions sometimes ask the corporate headquarters why it incurs a large amount of corporate costs. To deal with this question, the corporate headquarters should spend money efficiently and have a reasonable allocation system. Traditionally, it is said that people in the United States think the responsibility should match with authority and managers must be responsible only for controllable events. However, even in the United States, many researchers have entertained doubts about this theory.[6] Simons (2005) proposes the concept of shared responsibilities that are "the obligations that individuals assume to help others who are working toward shared goals" (Simons, 2005, p. 166), even though they are not responsible for these tasks. In addition, this point has been emphasized by Simons (2010). This allocation system promotes interaction between the corporate headquarters and divisions. The mutual check-and-balance system is also called one type of social control system, and it is said that this system is effective, especially in Japanese companies.

Second, although some of the corporate costs are uncontrollable for division managers, they must be recovered by division profits. Thus division managers should know how much division profits they need.

Third, when division managers know what an allocation base (cost driver) is, they start to try to decrease the consumption of corporate services. In many cases, when divisions consume corporate services, corporate costs are incurred. Therefore, if divisions would like to decrease the amount of allocated costs, division managers should consider the appropriate amount of corporate services for the respective divisions.

The last theme of this section is how to allocate corporate costs. The criteria for selecting an allocation base include (1) the received benefits criterion, (2) the cause and effect criterion, and (3) the ability to bear criterion. When companies find the cause and effect relationship between corporate costs and resources used by each division, criterion (2) must be used. When the cause and effect relationship is not clear but divisions receive benefits from corporate services, the received benefits criterion is used. In other cases, companies use the ability to bear criterion.

Even Japanese textbooks suggest that the ABC system should be used for allocating corporate costs when there is a cause and effect relationship. However, this relationship is difficult to find in many cases. The research shows that only 7.3 percent of companies in the non-manufacturing industry and 5.6 percent in the manufacturing industry in Japan use ABC for allocating corporate costs (Yoshida et al., 2012, p. 107).

This research indicates that nearly 80 percent of Japanese companies divide corporate costs into some cost pools and use the allocation base proper for each cost pool (Yoshida et al., 2012, p. 107). According to my interview survey, many companies actually use sales and the number of employees as an allocation base. When corporate costs are divided into some cost pools, the allocation becomes complicated and division managers begin negotiating with the headquarters for a smaller amount of allocation of corporate costs to their divisions. Some of the Japanese companies in the survey used many cost pools once, but some of these companies returned an allocation base to sales because the calculation of allocation was too complicated for them to understand what allocation base they should control.

10. How to evaluate managers of decentralized organizations in Japan

I pointed out earlier that income statements of divisions are different between the United States and Japan. However, it does not mean that the way of measuring division performance is different. Japanese companies tend to measure division performance by income before tax because it is the income after subtracting all costs from revenues and shows the bottom line.

On the other hand, according to U.S. textbooks, companies tend to use division profits to measure division performance. Division managers are required to make positive division profits at the minimum. Also, they are required to earn a surplus to cover corporate costs. It is almost the same as the Japanese system, in which division managers are required to make net income before tax. Although the U.S. system and the Japanese system are apparently different, they may have almost the same effect of making company-wide profits.

Notes

1 Panasonic abolished the division system in 2000 but revived it in 2013.
2 Corporate assets may be allocated to divisions or may be owned by a central office.
3 Even in a functional system, when each division or department is set as a profit center, this income statement can be used.
4 This research was conducted in 2009 (Yoshida et al., 2012). They sent out questionnaires to 856 companies in the non-manufacturing sector listed on the first section of the Tokyo Stock Exchange and 851 ones in the manufacturing sector. The response rate was 14.8 percent(127) in the non-manufacturing sector and 17.7 percent(151) in the manufacturing sector.
5 For example, the result of the research by Tani (1987) shows that 85 percent of the respondents allocated corporate costs to divisions.
6 See Horngren (1967), Merchant (1989), and Welsh et al. (1988).

References

Chandler, A. (1962) *Strategy and Structure: Chapters in the History of the Industrial Enterprise*, Boston, MA: MIT Press.

Horngren, C.T. (1967) *Cost Accounting: A Managerial Emphasis*, 2nd edition, Englewood Cliffs, NJ: Prentice Hall.

Horngren, C.T., S.M. Datar, and M. Rajan (2012) *Cost Accounting: A Managerial Emphasis*, 14th edition, Upper Saddle River, NJ: Prentice Hall.

Kobayashi, Y. (2009) Management accounting in decentralized organizations, in Kobayashi, Y., Y. Ito, T. Shimizu, and K. Hasegawa (eds.) *Standard Management Accounting*, Chapter 13, pp. 440–471, Tokyo, Japan: Toyo Keizai Inc. Written in Japanese.

Merchant, K.A. (1989) *Rewarding Results: Motivating Profit Center Managers*, Boston, MA: Harvard Business School Press.

Simons, R. (2005) *Levers of Organization Design: How Managers Use Accountability Systems for Greater Performance and Commitment*, Boston, MA: Harvard Business School Press.

Simons, R. (2010) *Seven Strategy Questions: A Simple Approach for Better Execution*, Boston, MA: Harvard Business School Publishing.

Tani, T. (1987) *The Measurement and Control of the Performance of Divisions*, Tokyo, Japan: Zeimu-Keiri Kyokai. Written in Japanese.

Yoshida, E., K. Fukushima, and T. Senoo (2012) *The Investigation of Japanese Management Accounting*, Tokyo, Japan: Chuokeizai-sha Inc. Written in Japanese.

Welsh, G.A., R.W. Hilton, and P.N. Gordon (1988) *Budgeting: Profit-Planning and Control*, 5th edition, Englewood Cliffs, NJ: Prentice Hall.

6 Balanced Scorecard versus the Japanese system

Key learning points

- The Balanced Scorecard is the tool of strategic management system and is used globally.
- The Balanced Scorecard is constructed with the Strategy Map and Scorecard. The Strategy Map has strategic objectives that show the path to execute a strategy The Scorecard has measures, targets, and strategic initiatives to implement strategic objectives.
- In Japan, the percentage of the companies that use BSC is small. It is related to Japanese traditional management ideas and tools, especially Hoshin-Kanri. You will learn about Hoshin-Kanri in this chapter.

1. Introduction

From the latter half of the 20th century through the 21st century, one of the most successful management tools is the Balanced Scorecard (BSC). It is a strategic management tool developed by Kaplan and Norton and enables companies to fully implement a formulated business strategy. Kaplan and Norton have already published five books regarding the BSC, all of which are best sellers (Kaplan and Norton, 1996; 2001; 2002; 2006; 2008). Many companies around the world use BSC, and it seems to be de facto standard. Dozens of books bearing titles that include the phrase "Balanced Scorecard" have also been published in Japan.

Also, many management accounting textbooks published in various countries include the BSC as the topic of at least one important chapter, and therefore the BSC should be a vital tool for business management. However, how many Japanese companies have adopted it? As stated later, the rate of BSC use in Japan is extremely low, even though the BSC is recognized as a standard management tool. I think there are two reasons for this: One reason is that Japanese companies have the same management thought as the BSC. The other reason is that Japanese companies have some alternatives to the BSC, such as Hoshin-Kanri and management by objectives. In this chapter, I (1) explain what the BSC is, (2) explain the state of BSC adoption in Japan, (3) describe the basic idea of management in Japanese companies, and (4) explain *Hoshin-Kanri* as a tool for implementing strategy in Japanese companies.

2. What is the Balanced Scorecard?

The Balanced Scorecard is a strategic management tool to implement a formulated strategy and sometimes to fine-tune or improve this strategy. Based on the business strategy, organizations can decide the strategic objectives, build the logic of strategy execution, and translate business strategies into action. Companies draw strategy maps to show logical strategy execution courses through four perspectives: financial, customer, internal process, and learning and growth.

The basic concept of the BSC is very simple (see Figure 6.1). At first, companies need to decide a financial goal to satisfy shareholders and investors. This goal is shown in the *Financial Perspective*. In the financial perspective, there are two dimensions: revenue growth and productivity improvement. As is commonly understood, companies can make better profits when companies earn more revenues and cut costs.

To attain their financial goal, especially in view of revenue growth, companies must sell their products and services to customers at appropriate prices. To do that, companies need to decide targeted customers and make some value

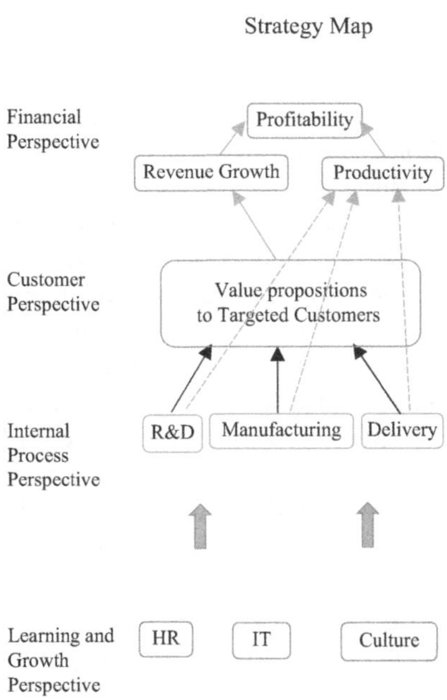

Scorecard

Strategic objective	Measure	Target	Strategic Initiative
Profitability	ROI	**	
Revenue Growth	***	**	
Productivity	***	**	
CS	CS Index	**	******************
***	***	**	******************
***	***	**	******************
R&D	***	**	******************
Cost	***	**	******************
Delivery time	***	**	******************
HR	***	**	******************
IT	***	**	******************
Culture	***	**	******************

Figure 6.1 The components of Balanced Scorecard

propositions to generate targeted customers' satisfaction. These strategic objectives are shown in the *Customer Perspective.*

To satisfy their customers, companies need to have an excellent process of manufacturing and/or delivering their products and services. These strategic objectives are shown in the *Internal Process Perspective.*

To have an excellent internal process, companies need to have good intangibles, which are capable employees (human resources); information technology to assist in making good decisions; and culture to activate organizations. These strategic objectives are shown in the *Learning and Growth Perspective.*

However, because strategic objectives are depictive – for example, "increase customer value" in the customer perspective – employees do not know what to do. Therefore, a measure to evaluate the progress of action plans called strategic initiatives, a target of the measure, and some strategic initiatives to implement strategic objectives must be set for each strategic objective. This relationship is shown in the Scorecard. Thus, BSCs consist of strategy maps that give a logical explanation of business strategy execution and scorecards that explain how to implement strategic objectives in strategy maps.

These vertical and horizontal cause and effect chains are shown in Figure 6.1.

3. The structure of the strategy map and the scorecard

Strategy map

As shown in Figure 6.1, the Strategy Map represents the vertical cause and effect chain of strategic objectives through four perspectives. Companies need to make an effective strategy to meet shareholders' and investors' expectations. To do that, companies must propose good value to their customers.

Kaplan and Norton offer three value propositions: product leadership, customer intimacy, and operational excellence (Kaplan and Norton, 2001, pp. 86–87).[1] In the value proposition of product leadership, companies develop and make excellent products and services for which people are willing to pay a lot of money. In Japan, Sony had this strategy for the Walkman once. In customer intimacy, companies understand their customers and make strong connections with them. Luxury hotels employ this strategy. Many companies use the reward card system and make good connections with their customers by analyzing their purchasing activities and offering fascinating goods and services to them. In operational excellence, companies give customers the best price for products of moderate quality. In other words, the price is lower than that in other companies that sell the same quality of goods and services. UNIQLO is a typical example. However, UNIQLO has been launching a lot of new fabric products jointly developed with Toray, a leading company in the textile industry. It seems that UNIQLO has been striving to become a product leadership company. Kaplan and Norton (1996) pointed out that companies must select only one value proposition, but that is not suitable for Japanese companies. Many companies in Japan struggle to propose good value at lower cost or to be intimate with customers at lower cost. In the Japanese market, customers expect companies to offer products with the best quality and functionality at reasonable prices and to provide the best service for nothing. Japanese companies need to meet all these expectations. This causes intense competition among Japanese companies. They compete on all sides of price, functionality, and quality. Cooper and Slagmulder (1999) called this "confrontation strategy." While this surely led to Japanese companies' growth, it caused over-quality. The following is often pointed out. Although Japanese products have high quality and multi-function, they far exceed the real needs of customers. Companies incur over-costs to ensure over-quality and over-functionality, and these costs need transferring to customers. However, customers would not like to pay high costs, and companies cannot gain acceptable returns. This situation is one of the problems Japanese manufacturers have. Japanese companies must consider whether they should keep competing on all sides of price, function, and quality, or provide products and services with moderate quality and functionality for targeted customers.

Let us get back to strategic objectives. In any case, companies must focus some factors on satisfying their customers. These factors are "strategic objectives". In each strategy (value proposition), the objectives are necessary to exercise the cause and effect chain.

Figure 6.2 shows a strategy map of a hypothetical case of a restaurant in Japan. The vision of this restaurant is *to provide enjoyable meals for three-generation families.* To attain this vision, it focuses on three factors: expansion of customer base, increase in revenues per customer, and reduction in costs per customer in the financial perspective. In the four perspectives, the vital factors for strategy execution are called strategic objectives, which are shown within the ovals in Figure 6.2. In the customer perspective, this company has five strategic objectives to attain two financial strategic objectives (to expand customer base and to increase revenues per customer). In the internal process perspective, it chooses seven strategic objectives to attain one financial strategic objective (to reduce costs per customer) and five strategic objectives in the customer perspective. Finally, the strategic objectives in the learning and growth perspective are at the base of the strategy map. This relationship among strategic objectives is the vertical cause and effect chain.[2]

Scorecard

A strategy map shows the logic of strategy execution and tells it to all employees. However, even though employees know the outline or the logic of strategy execution, they do not know specifically what to do. The BSC is intended to make a strategy for daily actions. The next step is to consider specific actions to attain each strategic objective.

A strategic initiative is a specific action that is taken by employees. For example, you can see "Improve the quality of side dishes, beverages, and desserts" in Figure 6.2. Most side dishes, beverages, and desserts are prepared by hall staff. Their quality is critical to obtain the satisfaction of customers who come to this restaurant at teatime. To attain this objective, this company

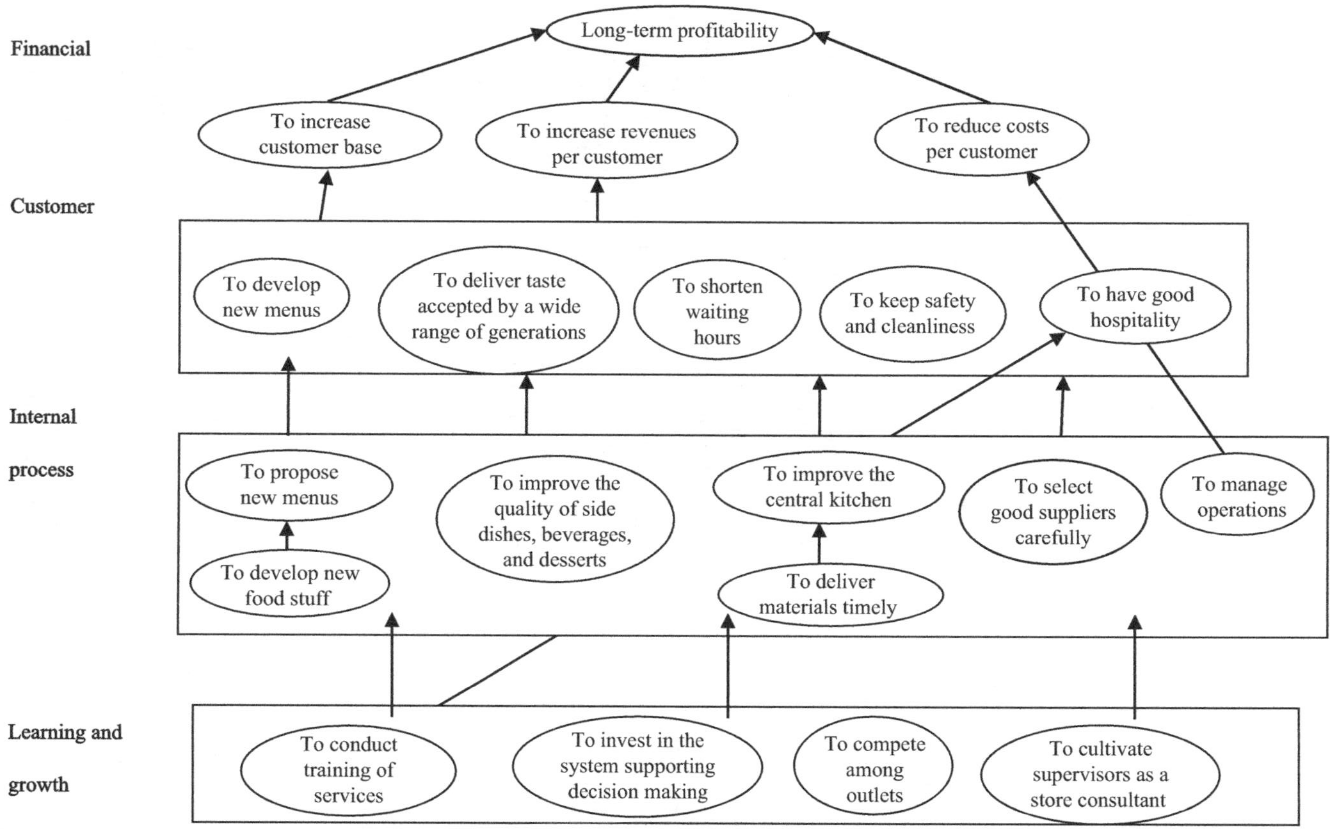

Figure 6.2 The strategy map of a chain restaurant company

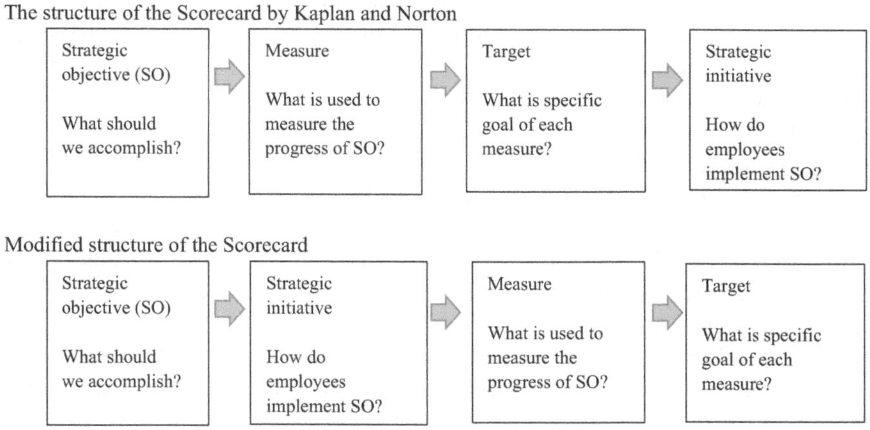

Figure 6.3 The structure of the scorecard

considers two strategic initiatives. One is the development of ways to serve dessert decoratively on dishes at the central kitchen, and the other is its training. It is not until employees are presented with these action plans that they understand their strategy and put it into action.

Once managers understand strategic initiatives, they decide measures (metric, index, or standard) to measure the progress of strategic initiatives. Managers select measures that they have already used if these measures are appropriate to measure the progress of the strategic initiative. If not, they must set new measures. Finally, managers have to set a goal for each measure. This relationship is called “the horizontal cause and effect chain” (Shimizu, 2013).

Kaplan and Norton (2000) suggest that first measures are decided, then targets are set, and then strategic initiatives are considered. In my experiences of helping some Japanese companies introduce the BSC, this order has not worked well because managers often expend all their energy on finding measures and setting targets. I saw many managers be enthusiastic about finding measures and deciding targets without considering how to achieve strategic objectives.

Of course “strategic initiatives” are the most important in accomplishing strategic objectives. Therefore, I have proposed to some managers that they should consider strategic initiatives right after thinking out strategic objectives, and that they should find appropriate measures and targets. This modified structure of the scorecard is shown in Figure 6.3.

4. The actual state of the adoption of BSCs in Japan

From the late 1990s to the early 2000s, some Japanese companies adopted a new strategic management system, the BSC. Ricoh, a manufacturer of copy machines and printers, started to make a study of the possibility of using the BSC in 1999.[3] Ricoh was awarded the Japan Quality Award[4] (JQA) in 1999 and went into action to integrate its budgeting system, JQA, and Hoshin-Kanri into the new strategic management by objectives (i.e., the BSC). Ricoh was enshrined in the Hall of Fame for Executing Strategy in 2005. Bank of Tokyo-Mitsubishi (BTM)[5] introduced the BSC in 2000 (Kaplan and Norton, 2004). It has been using the BSC for more than 15 years and was enshrined in the Hall of Fame of the BSC in 2007. They are notably successful cases in using BSCs. Also some other large companies, such as Kirin Brewery,[6] Fuji Xerox, and Kansai Electric Power introduced BSCs.

However, I cannot say that BSCs are used by many Japanese companies now. Some researchers conducted questionnaire surveys concerning the use of BSCs. The recent survey by Kawano (2014) shows the percentage of companies using BSCs is 8.2 percent. Some companies that adopted BSCs before have stopped using them lately.

On the other hand, there are interesting results of surveys. I was asked by the Centre for Business Performance of Cranfield University in the United Kingdom to conduct a survey of enterprise performance management in Japan in 2006. It was also conducted in the United States, the United Kingdom, China, and Australia (Neely et al., 2008). In this survey, 44.7 percent of the respondents answered that they used BSCs. This number is much higher than the results of other surveys. However, not all of these companies introduced BSCs in a complete form. The percentage of using strategy maps was only 10.7 percent, and the percentage of companies understanding the cause and effect relationship among performance measures was 9.7 percent (Shimizu, 2013, pp. 46–47). Why is there a big difference in percentage? Do Japanese companies use BSCs or not? In conclusion, the percentage of Japanese companies that use formal BSCs, strategy maps, and scorecards is low, but the idea of BSCs has penetrated many companies. There are two reasons why the idea of BSCs became widespread. First, Japanese companies have a strong belief that they must treasure many kinds of stakeholders, such as customers, suppliers, and employees. Second, they have a similar management system to the BSC, called *Hoshin-Kanri.*

5. The basic idea of management in Japanese companies

Abegglen (1958) introduced the Japanese management style. In his book, he introduced some features of the employment system in Japan, such as lifetime employment, seniority-based wages, in-house training, and company union system. They are so famous that there seems to be no need to explain them. It is clear that these features have strengthened the Japanese economy for dozens of years. Here I will focus on two features.

First, many Japanese people have perceived their companies as their family. In Japan, we often use the phrase "familistic management" or "management by big familism." This means that a company must sustain employees like their father and employees work together for a company like its children to help their parents. Although Japanese society has been changing slowly from big familism to privatism, the concept of the familistic management style still remains about the same.

A company ensures long-term employment and a pay rise. Employees commit themselves to working for company's profits. In addition to long-term employment and a continuous pay rise, companies offer several additional incentives. For example, some companies had luxurious facilities at popular tourist destinations and the hotel charges were inexpensive, a half or one-third of market price. After the 1980s some companies sold these facilities, but even now there are many facilities that companies own. Besides these things, they have many health care plans and recreational plans to allow employees to have a good time.

Companies needed these systems to encourage their employees to catch up with the Western world after World War II. The systems led Japanese companies to have a strong corporate culture of cooperation and collaboration. In brief, Japanese companies have long been familiar with the BSC concepts "organizational capital" and "human capital."

Second, a main stakeholder is a customer. Companies believe that customers are most important for their operations. "The customer is always right" or "the customer is king" is a phrase that we can see all over the world, and in Japan we say "the customer is god." Although these are similar phrases, there is a difference in the way of thinking about customers between the United States and Japan. While in the United States targeted customers are often set clearly, in Japan all people that purchase products and services are customers and gods. Thus companies serve customers as much as possible. For example, let us consider store hours. Assume that the closing hour of a shop is seven o'clock. Guess what happens at seven o'clock. In the United States, the last clerk locks the door and leaves the shop at seven. In Japan, the last customer can enter the shop at seven. This is based on customer-centric philosophy.

However, this idea causes over-quality, as I mentioned before, because companies try to give all customers a feeling of satisfaction. The needs of customers are widely spread. A feature may match one customer's expectation, but it may not match the expectation of others. If companies respond to all of the customers' needs, too many features are built-in the products and it costs too much. This is a problem in Japanese companies.

To serve customers, of course, Japanese companies know that they should have excellent internal processes even though they do not have the BSC theory. They have been improving their manufacturing processes continuously to cut costs. This is well known as "Kaizen." Japanese companies have excellent internal processes in the product development area as well as in the manufacturing area. Target costing was developed by assembly manufacturers such as Toyota, Nissan, and Panasonic. Its goal is to develop products that attract many customers at low cost. Thus, in essence Japanese companies have worked on customer-centric development and manufacturing systems.

When BSCs were introduced in the 1990s, I had interviews with some top managers of large companies. Some answered that the BSC was a very interesting management idea but that they already had the same way of thinking as BSCs for many years. In my opinion, there are two reasons why BSCs are not used by many Japanese companies. One is that Japanese companies have had a basic idea similar to BSCs for a long time, and have no necessity to adopt BSCs. BSCs include some features of Japanese companies' way of thinking on management. Therefore, as companies in Japan understood BSCs better, more companies that had adopted BSCs decided to abandon the system. The other reason is that Japanese companies have had the same kind of "management tool" as BSCs, called *Hoshin-Kanri.*

6. Hoshin-Kanri

Definition and features

Hoshin-Kanri was generated by TQM (Total Quality Management). TQM means raising the quality of management. It is a customer-focused and quality-focused management style. Quality includes three factors: quality of products and services, quality of processes of manufacturing and delivering products and services, and quality of the processes of up-skilling employees.

While this TQM was developing, Hoshin-Kanri has made progress in Japan since the 1960s. Hoshin-Kanri is defined as follows:

> Hoshin-Kanri is the activities to create long-term or medium-term management plans based on corporate mission and to efficiently accomplish these plans with company-wide cooperation.
>
> (The Subcommittee of Discussion of the Terminology of TQC, 1988, p. 47, translated from Japanese)

In Japan, mission is often expressed as Sha-ze, Sha-kun, Keiei-Rinen. It shows corporate philosophy (the basic idea on management in a company) and basic principles to pursue corporate philosophy. However, it is so hard to have specific plans if companies have only a vague mission. Thus they have to formulate long-term or medium-term management plans (The Subcommittee of Discussion of the Terminology of TQC, 1988, p. 48, translated from Japanese).

Flow of Hoshin-Kanri

The flow of Hoshin-Kanri is shown in Figure 6.4. Companies have their mission. It shows the significance of existence or raison d'être of the company to keep pursuing. A mission is usually obscure or subjective. Therefore, companies must have their specific medium-term goal. In the BSC theory, a medium-term goal is "vision." Next, they need to formulate a medium-term management plan to achieve it. It is often called "strategy."

Once the strategy is formulated, companies make a short-term management plan. It has specific objectives and Hosaku (an action plan) to accomplish these objectives.

Objectives are set in all functional departments. They cover a wide field such as profits, production volume, sales, costs, quality, and delivery time.

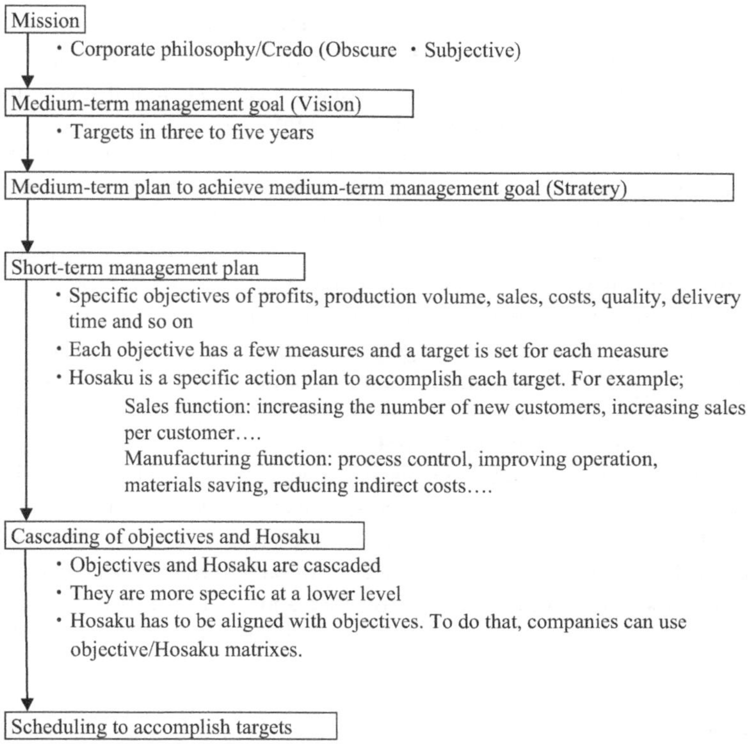

Figure 6.4 The flow of Hoshin-Kanri

Each objective has measures and targets. For example, sales departments often have objectives of sales, costs, and sales quality. Manufacturing departments often have objectives of the quality of products, manufacturing costs, and delivery time.

Hosaku is a specific action plan to accomplish targets in objectives. One or two Hosaku are set for each objective.

The next step is cascading. Cascading is a word used in BSC theory. It is defined as the process of developing Balanced Scorecards at lower levels of an organization (Niven, 2005, p. 128). In the theory of Hoshin-Kanri, the meaning of cascading is totally the same as that of BSCs. In a sales department, a general sales manager has his/her own objective on sales. The measure of this objective is usually the amount of sales – for example, the target is five billion yen. This target is cascaded to the target of each branch chief and its target is cascaded to the target of each manager. Hosaku is also cascaded. That is to say, company-wide targets and Hosaku are cascaded to various levels of a company from top management to lower managers.

Comparison of Hoshin-Kanri and BSCs

As stated previously, there are many similarities between Hoshin-Kanri and BSCs. Both of them use the same words or the same concepts: mission, strategy, objectives, measures, targets, strategic initiatives (Hosaku), and cascading. The framework of these tools is also almost the same.

Hoshin-Kanri was introduced in the 1960s, and it is so similar to BSCs. In fact, Ito points out that U.S. researchers conducted exhaustive research into Japanese management system during the 1980s and BSCs were therefore much influenced by Hoshin-Kanri (Ito, 2001, p. 47). This is one of the reasons that Japanese companies have not introduced BSCs.

However, Hoshin-Kanri has some differences from the BSC. First, Hoshin-Kanri is a tool of short-term management rather than a tool of strategic management. The BSC is set under a specific strategy and communicates it to all employees to execute it properly. On the other hand, Hoshin-Kanri may not postulate as clear a strategy as the BSC.

Second, Hoshin-Kanri cascades each single objective, whereas in the BSC theory, a set of objectives in four perspectives is cascaded. In other words, Hoshin-Kanri does not clearly have multiple perspectives. However, the target in Hoshin-Kanri – for example, the objective of sales in the financial perspective – is directly linked with objectives in customer and internal process perspectives. Consequently, the forms of Hoshin-Kanri and the BSC are different, but the concepts are virtually the same.

Third, the BSC explicitly has four stakeholders at least in its system but in the Hoshin-Kanri theory Japanese companies implicitly consider customers, employees, creditors, and society, as mentioned before. Japanese companies have known that the balance of the four BSC perspectives is extremely important since even before the official introduction of BSC.

Now many Japanese companies are expanding their business overseas. Each host country has a different way of thinking and different national culture from those in Japan. Apart from internal subsidiaries, Japanese companies must tell all employees at overseas subsidiaries what their strategy is, who their targeted customers are, which value proposition they offer to those customers, what products and services they deliver to those customers, and how they make products. Therefore, companies should introduce the BSC explicitly when they expand their business worldwide.

Notes

1 Kaplan and Norton (2004, pp. 49–51) revised value propositions from the previous three ones to the following four ones: minimum total cost, product leadership, perfect customer solution, and system lock-in. I think that the latter two ones are included in customer intimacy.
2 Some researchers point out that this relationship in the strategy map is not the cause and effect chain in a strict sense (Nørreklit, 2000).
3 For further details, see Itoh (2001a; Chapter 4).

4 The Japan Quality Award is a Japanese version of the Malcom Baldrige National Quality Award.
5 At that time, BTM introduced the BSC into the U.S. headquarters. BTM and UFJ Bank merged into Bank of Tokyo-Mitsubishi UFJ in 2006.
6 Now it is a subsidiary of Kirin Holdings Company.

References

Abegglen, J. (1958) *The Japanese Factory*, New York, NY: Basic Books.

Cooper, R. and R. Slagmulder (1999) *Supply Chain Development for the Lean Enterprise: Interorganizational Cost Management*, Portland, OR: Productivity Press.

Itoh, Y. (2001a) Strategic management by objectives, the case of Ricoh, in Itoh, Y., T. Shimizu, and K. Hasegawa (eds.) *Theory and Practice of Balanced Scorecard*, Chapter 4, pp. 76–100, Tokyo, Japan: Daiamondo-sha. Written in Japanese.

Kaplan, R.S. and D.P. Norton (1996) *The Balanced Scorecard: Translating Strategy into Action*, Boston, MA: Harvard School Business Press.

Kaplan, R.S. and D.P. Norton (2000) *The Strategy Focused Organization: How Balanced Scorecard Companies Thrive in the New Business Environment*, Boston, MA: Harvard School Business Press.

Kaplan, R.S. and D.P. Norton (2004) *Strategy Maps: Converting Intangible Asset into Tangible Outcome*, Boston, MA: Harvard School Business Press.

Kaplan, R.S. and D.P. Norton (2006) *Alignment: Using the Balanced Scorecard to Create Corporate Synergies*, Boston, MA: Harvard School Business Press.

Kaplan, R.S. and D.P. Norton (2008) *Execution Premium: Linking Strategy to Operations for Competitive Advantage*, Boston, MA: Harvard School Business Press.

Kawano, K. (2014) The present situation and problems of the management accounting and the cost accounting of the Japanese companies, *The Study of Business and Industry* (College of Commerce, Nihon University), 30, 55–86.

Morisawa, T., H. Miyata, and H. Kurosaki (2005) *Management by Balanced Scorecard*, Tokyo, Japan: Nikkei Inc. Written in Japanese.

Neely, A., B. Yaghi, and N. Youell (2008) *Enterprise Performance Management: The Global State of the Arts*, Oracle and Cranfield School of Management.

Niven, P. (2005) *Balanced Scorecard Diagnostics: Maintaining Maximum Performance*, Hoboken, NJ: John Wiley & Sons.

Nørreklit, H. (2000) The balance on the balanced scorecard: A critical analysis of some of its assumptions, *Management Accounting Research*, 11(1), 65–88.

Shimizu, T. (2013) *Performance Management to Implement the Business Strategy*, Tokyo, Japan: Chuokeizai-sha Inc. Written in Japanese.

The Subcommittee of Discussion of the terminology of TQC (1988) Definition of check items, Ho-shin kanri, Nichijo kanri, functional control, and management by division, *Quality Management*, 39(3), Union of Japanese Scientists and Engineers, 47–50. Written in Japanese.

7 Performance measures

ROI, ROS, ROE, and EVA®

Key learning points

- Learn four major financial performance measures: ROI, ROS, ROE, and EVA®
- Why do Japanese companies place importance on sales and amount of profits?
- What should Japanese companies do to improve their ROE?

1. Introduction

Whether the BSC is used or not, a financial measure is highly important to management control. That is because the final goal is to make profits in most performance measurement systems. Needless to say, a profit is the difference between revenues and costs. In business, companies must sell products and services as much as possible by hundreds of actions generating costs. The goal is, therefore, to maximize sales and minimize costs. Figure 7.1 shows a sample of business structure.

First, companies raise funds from investors (direct financing) or creditors (indirect financing) such as a bank. Next, they purchase assets to make money. They also hire employees and lease stores. As a result, costs are incurred. Companies make good action plans that attract customers. They make efforts to develop good products, to have lean processes to make products, to boost product quality, and to deliver products quickly. They earn revenues from their business by activities that incur costs. The balance between revenues and costs is profits. Companies gain profits and retain earnings to invest in future plans. At the same time, they must repay principal and interest to creditors and make returns from their business to satisfy the expected rate of returns for shareholders.

In this basic structure, the cycle is as follows: investors and creditors invest in companies, the companies invest in their business, and they must earn enough returns to pay interests and to live up to shareholders' expectations.

Thus, companies focus on financial measures, such as return on investment (ROI), return on equity (ROE), and economic value added (EVA®). I will explain these in the next three sections.

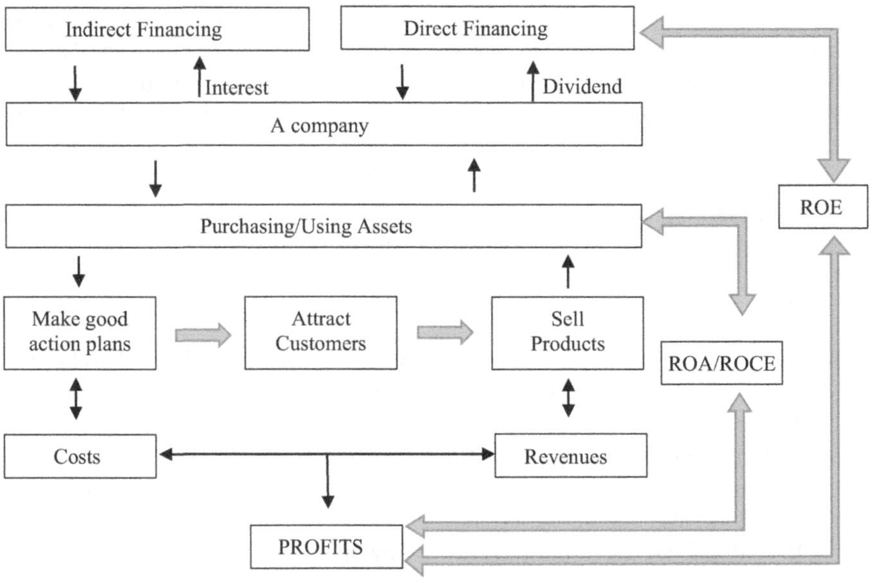

Figure 7.1 Business structure

2. Return on investment

To measure investment efficiency, we use ROI, which is calculated as net income divided by investment:

$$\text{ROI}(\%) = \frac{\textit{Net Income}(\textit{Profit})}{\textit{Investment}} = \frac{\textit{Net Income}}{\textit{Sales}}(ROS) \times \frac{\textit{Sales}}{\textit{Investment}}(CT)$$

As shown in Figure 7.1, companies invest raised money in their business to earn profits. That is to say, investment is "input" and profit is "return." Companies must earn a suitable return on their investment.

Generally, ROI is composed of two factors – return on sales (ROS) and capital turnover (CT). ROS is the percentage of profits to sales, and it shows the profitability of a company. Capital turnover is the percentage of sales to investments. As we understand through this formula, to increase ROI, companies need to increase ROS or capital turnover. In general, when companies increase revenues keeping investment constant, capital turnover rises. However, ROS decreases if revenues increase without increasing profits. In this case, the decline in ROS absolutely sets off the increase of capital turnover. Consequently, companies must increase profits or decrease investments to improve ROI.

Investment in ROI means "the amount invested," and we find it both on the debit side and on the credit side of a balance sheet. We find there are many asset items on the debit side of a balance sheet. They show a company's investment amount in its business. Thus, focusing on the debit side, the sum of investment amount from shareholders and borrowings from creditors is equal to the total assets. In this case, the measure is called return on assets (ROA). When companies have unused assets for a business, they can use return on capital employed (ROCE) by dividing net income by capital employed (total assets – unused assets).

On the other hand, focusing on the credit side, an investment is equal to the sum of liabilities and capital. In this case, to calculate ROI, we should use Earnings before Income and Tax (EBIT), not operating income. EBIT is calculated as follows:

$$\text{EBIT} = \text{Net Income before Tax} + \text{Interest}$$

EBIT is income that a company earns by using all funds from shareholders and creditors. The net income is attributable to shareholders, and it does not include the return to creditors, or interest. An appropriate concept of income here includes the return from all funds. Also interest income and dividends income that a company earns from investment in financial assets are required to be included in EBIT, because they are the return from total funds of a company.

ROS and CT are decomposed into many sub-factors. ROS is decomposed into gross profit on sales, operating income margin, and the like. Capital turnover is composed of current assets turnover and fixed assets turnover. The former is composed of inventory turnover, accounts receivable turnover, and the like in the asset side. They are useful measures to make a diagnosis of the profitability of a company.

3. Return on equity

ROE is a measure that shows the percentage of net income to the amount invested by shareholders. Recently ROE has been seen as the most important measure to investors. ROE is calculated as net income divided by net assets.

$$\text{ROE} = \frac{Net\ Income}{Net\ Assets} = \frac{Net\ Income}{Revenue}(ROS) \times \frac{Revenue}{Total\ Assets}(CT) \times \frac{Total\ Assets}{Net\ Assets}(Leverage)$$

ROE is the product of three items: ROS, capital turnover, and leverage. ROS and CT have already been explained. Leverage means that using borrowed capital increases volatility (ROE fluctuations). To put it simply, decreasing net assets by increasing debts has a positive effect of improving ROE.

Although there are three ways of improving ROE: increasing ROS, CT, and leverage, as explained earlier, CT increased by increasing revenues is totally set off by decreasing ROS. Consequently, there are only two ways of improving ROE effectively: improving ROS by earning more net income and using leverage. However, companies should be careful about using high leverage because of the associated risks.

In addition, ROE is composed of two parts: earnings per share (EPS) and book value per share (BPS).

$$\text{ROE} = \frac{\textit{Net Income}}{\textit{Number of Common Share Issued}}(\textit{EPS})$$
$$\div \frac{\textit{Shareholder Equity}}{\textit{Number of Common Share Issued}}(\textit{BPS})$$

4. Economic value added®

Economic Value Added (EVA®) was introduced by Stern Stewart & Co. in the 1990s (Stewart, G. B. III, 1990). It is the same concept as residual income.[1] According to Stewart, EVA® is one of the most suitable metrics for measuring corporate value. The difference of EVA® from ROI and ROE is that EVA® is the amount, while ROI and ROE are the proportion. The larger the scale of investment, the bigger EVA® is. A company may improve ROI by decreasing total capital or improve ROE by decreasing net assets. In these cases, ROI and ROE are improved, but these approaches may lead this company to reproduction on a regression scale. We can check the expansion of scale by EVA® and the capital efficiency by ROI or ROE.

Although EVA® needs a very complex adjustment calculation, we can obtain the approximate value of EVA® by the following formula.[2]

EVA® = Net Operating Profit after Tax (NOPAT) – Capital Charge
Capital Charge (Cost of Capital) = Weighted Average Capital Cost × Economic Capital Employed
Economic Capital Employed = Total Capital – Non-Interest-Bearing Current Liabilities

NOPAT is based on profits after tax earned from companies' operations, and it is the base of the return to shareholders. Capital charge is the cost of companies' funds. When companies raise money from creditors or investors, they incur costs – for example, interest and dividends.

Capital charge is calculated as the product of weighted average capital cost (WACC) and economic capital employed. The formula provided has been simplified to make it more accessible. In fact, the calculation of economic capital employed is very complex, and many textbooks explain that the amounts of marketable securities and construction account should be deducted.

The cost of debt is interest that a company must pay to creditors when it borrows money. Companies easily know interest of new borrowing. When they produce corporate bonds, the yield to maturity is the cost of debt.

On the other hand, the cost of equity is a little difficult to presume. There are some ways of calculating this, but I will explain the most popular method, capital asset pricing model (CAPM). In the CAPM model, the expected rate of return of individual stocks ($E(R_i)$) is calculated by using the following formula:[3]

$$E(R_i) = R_f + \beta(E(R_M) - R_f)$$

where

R_f is the risk-free rate of interest from, for example, government bonds[4]
β is the coefficient of sensitivity, or the expected stock rate of return to the expected market rate of return
$E(R_M)$ is the expected rate of return of the stock market

The difference between the expected rate of return and the risk-free rate is called "risk premium," which investors require when they invest in risk assets. Based on the CAPM model, when we get the risk-free rate of interest, β, and the expected rate of return of the stock market, we can calculate the expected return of the stock of a company.

After getting the cost of debt and the cost of equity, we calculate weighted average capital cost. Be sure to know what the cost of debt (R_D) is before deducting corporate tax.[5]

$$\text{WACC} = \frac{D}{D+E} \times R_D(1-T) + \frac{E}{D+E} \times R_E$$

where

D is interest-bearing debts
E is total shareholder's equity
R_D is the cost of debt
R_E is the cost of equity
T is the corporate tax rate

5. Japanese companies' preference in financial measures and its reason

As shown in the previous section, companies should use ROI, ROE, and/or EVA®. We will now take a look at the status of the use of financial performance measures in Japan. Generally Japanese companies use just sales, operating income, and return on sales (operating income to sales). Table 7.1 is a review of some Japanese articles that cover financial measures in Japanese companies.

Japanese companies value profits (especially operating income) and sales. The amount is much more important than the percentage such as ROS, ROI, and ROE. The percentage of companies that use ROI and ROE has been dramatically increasing recently. Investment from foreign investors has been increasing. Now the percentage of foreign investors buying and selling shares in the Tokyo Stock Exchange (TSE) is more than 60 percent.[6] This makes Japanese companies turn the spotlight on ROI and/or ROE, the global standards of financial measures. However, companies using ROI and ROE as a financial goal are noticeably fewer than ones using sales or income.

Table 7.1 Financial measures that Japanese companies prefer

	Yokota et al. (2013)[7]	*Kawano (2014)*[8]	*The Life Insurance Association of Japan (2015)*[9]
Sales	6.18	69.1%	63.6%
Gross margin	N.A.	34.0%	N.A.
Operating income	6.74[10]	72.8%	69.6%[11]
Keijo-Rieki[12]	N.A.	51.2%	N.A.
ROS	6.26	20.4	50.1%
ROI	4.70[13]	26.5%[14]	16.1%[15]
ROE	N.A.	24.1%	39.7%
EVA®	4.66	3.1%	0.0%

Table 7.2 The status of the utilization of EVA® in major Japanese companies

Company name	*Introduction year*	*Name*	*Status*
ORIX	1997	OVA	There is no mention of OVA or EVA® on its website.
HOYA	1998	SVA	HOYA uses SVA and considers it very important. SVA = ATA × (ROIA – WACA)
KAO	1999	EVA®	KAO calculates EVA® even now but places less significance on it.
Panasonic	1999	CCM	There is no mention of CCM or EVA® on its website.
Sony	1999	Modified EVA®	Sony disuses it.
Kansai Electric Power	2000	PCA	KEP uses it.
Kirin	2001	KVA	The amount of bonuses paid to inside directors is linked to consolidated EVA® (2013 Annual Report).
Mitsubishi Corporation	2001	MCVA	MITSUBISHI CORPORATION uses it.
Toshiba	2002	TVC	Toshiba disuses it.

From the annual report of each company

There are also some companies using EVA®. Table 7.2 shows the status of the utilization of EVA® in major companies. In the 1990s, there were many feature issues of accounting journals about EVA®, and there is no doubt EVA® attracted considerable attention of top management at that time. Why haven't Japanese companies used EVA®, ROI, and ROE?

In terms of Japanese history, there are some reasons for it, and the main reason is that Japanese companies have placed less significance on shareholders.

6. The reason why Japanese companies place less importance on shareholders

Historical background

Japan tried catching up with the Western world after having a closed-door policy for more than 200 years from the 17th to the 19th century. When the door was opened, technological competence in Japan was clearly inferior to that of Western countries. The Japanese government played a strong leadership role in the modernization of Japan. The government established many companies to develop key industries such as steel, mining, and textiles. Later, these companies were sold to some "Zaibatsu," a financial clique – for example, Mitsui, Mitsubishi and Sumitomo. Zaibatsu is a financial conglomerate owned by a family. They were the center of the Japanese economy before World War II, but they were dismantled by GHQ (General Headquarters of the Allied Forces). The most important thing was to catch up with the Western countries at that time. To do that, the government thought economic growth was essential, and protected some key industries to accelerate their growth. The protection of shareholders took a backseat to such protections. After World War II, the TSE opened in 1949[16] and the stock trade started again. Nevertheless, Japanese companies did not need to listen actively to their shareholders because of the financial structure centering on indirect finance and cross-shareholdings.

The financing structure centering on indirect finance

The government thought the indirect finance system was better than the direct finance system. The reason is that indirect finance made it easy to control the total amount of funds needed by companies. As noted before, the highest priority policy was consistently economic growth in modern history. Therefore, the government had to support companies that planned to raise money when they expanded their facility to make increasingly more products. It instituted "the convoy system" in the bank industry. By using this system, the government controlled all the banks and protected them from business collapse.

The turning point from indirect finance to direct finance was in the mid 1980s, the so-called bubble economy, and asset-inflated economy. Companies rushed into the equity and bond market to raise their funds. Because share prices skyrocketed and the bond market was liberalized, it was easy for companies to raise funds by the issuing of bonds and shares at lower cost than by borrowing. Companies have seriously considered their relationship with their shareholders since then.

Governance by banks (main-bank system)

The financial structure centering on indirect finance led most companies to adopt corporate governance by banks. Although companies do deals with some banks, companies mainly have a close relationship with only one bank. This is a main-bank system peculiar to Japanese companies. A main bank monitors its customer, who applies for a loan by reviewing customer's balance sheet, income statement, and cash flow statement. When the main bank finds something wrong with these financial statements, it does not give a loan to the customer. In the indirect finance system, if the main bank does not make loans to the company, the company runs short of cash. Companies did not have external corporate governance control because not shareholders but banks checked performance and management of companies. Companies focused on cash management and making a profit. In the remarkable growth of the Japanese economy, companies had only to focus on increasing sales because it brought high profits to them.

Cross-shareholdings

In addition to the main-bank system, cross-shareholdings led companies to leave shareholders out of the picture. Shares of a company are owned by a main bank, counterparties, and some companies that are incorporated into Keiretsu.[17] Especially companies that belong to Keiretsu have their shares owned by each other to protect them from hostile takeover. In this case, each company stays out of management in other companies because it also hopes other companies stay out of its management. Institutional investors regularly buy and sell shares of the targeted company, depending on its performance. However, cross-shareholding companies do not sell even though financial performance of an invested company becomes worse. Therefore, even though some investors make overtures to a company because they are frustrated with its performance and management, their overtures would not be adopted under the situation where cross-shareholders are in the majority.

As the impact of non-Japanese investors on the TSE became stronger, it became necessary for Japanese companies to improve the efficiency of capital. Cross-shareholdings make total assets excessive and are not an investment required by minor shareholders. Non-Japanese investors always point out that cross-shareholdings are unfair.

However, cross-shareholdings have been dissolving since the mid-1990s. As mentioned before, companies have been giving top priority to the efficiency of capital in order to draw support from foreign investors.

Regarding this, Japanese companies are reducing retained earnings by increasing dividends and share repurchase. Foreign investors often heavily criticize the fact that Japanese companies have excessive retained earnings. Based on the basic finance theory in the United States, companies must pay out more dividends when retained earnings are too high. However, Japanese companies tend not to do that and save retained earnings against emergencies. A retained earnings account is the credit account, and we do not know where retained earnings are invested. Japanese companies may have a lot of cash and its equivalent as an investment destination of retained earnings.

7. The actual status of Japanese companies' ROE

The Ministry of Economy, Trade and Industry (METI) formed the project named "Competitiveness and Incentives for Sustainable Growth: Building Favorable Relationships between Companies and Investors" in 2014. The report of this project was called the "Ito report" because the principal investigator was Professor Ito in Hitotsubashi University (METI, 2014). In this report, some recommendations with respect to this theme were made. One of them was a capital efficiency revolution. It means that ROE exceeds the cost of capital. This report shows that the ROE of Japanese companies is lower than that of other countries, and examines this low ROE (METI, 2014, pp. 50–52).

As mentioned before, ROE is broken down into three elements: ROS, CT, and Leverage. According to this report, ROE in the United States was 22.6 percent, that in Europe was 15.0 percent, and that in Japan was only 5.3 percent in 2012. The cause of low ROE in Japan can be found in low ROS. CT and Leverage in Japan were almost the same as those in the United States and Europe (METI, 2014, p. 37).

Yanagi (2015) shows the same result. He compared ROS, CT, and Leverage in Japanese companies with those in U.S. companies to explain why ROE in Japanese companies was so low (see Table 7.3). He found that although CT in Japan was almost the same as that in the United States, Leverage in Japan was higher than that in the United States. Thus the reason for low ROE in Japan was found in low ROS. Actually, the ROS of Japanese companies was less than half of that in U.S. companies.

8. Discussions

I think that many management control systems peculiar to Japan are meaningful and will have a beneficial influence on management in many countries. However, as far as Japanese companies tend to prefer the amount of sales, income, and ROS to ROI and ROE, I believe that Japanese companies must change their

Table 7.3 ROE, ROS, and CT in the United Kingdom, the United States, and Japan

	ROE	*ROS*	*CT*	*Leverage*[18]
U.K.	14.0%	7.2%	115%	59%
United States	13.8%	6.6%	118%	56%
Japan	5.6%	2.4%	125%	55%

Adapted from Yanagi (2015, pp. 40–44)

thinking if they hope to raise funds from international investors. And of course if companies in your country would like to do that, they should focus on ROI and ROE, too.

Now many Japanese companies have begun to regard ROE as a very important measure because they consider shareholders as important as customers and employees. Thus, what should they do? There are some avenues to this goal.

As I indicated previously, there are mainly three ways to improve ROE. The most important and hardest way is to improve ROS. Before that, I would like to mention the other two ways: improving CT and improving leverage. To improve CT, companies must reduce total assets or increase sales. Companies can repay a loan (decreasing assets as well as liabilities) or cancel shares (decreasing assets as well as net assets). These methods have an influence on leverage. The former leads to lower leverage and the latter leads to higher leverage.

High leverage is effective in gaining higher ROE. Thus methods of canceling shares and increasing dividends are often used. However, companies sometimes have high leverage by raising money by borrowing. In this case, the volatility of ROE increases, and this is not always good for companies and shareholders.

As a result, improving ROS is the healthiest way to increase ROE. In a sense, Japanese companies' approach is not bad.

The last problem in Japanese companies is why ROS is much lower than U.S. and European companies' ROS and what Japanese companies should do to improve it. There are some hypotheses to explain this phenomenon (but they are unproven). The most widely believed theory is that Japanese companies try to meet the needs of all customers at low prices. To satisfy their needs, products necessarily become over-quality at high cost. As shown in Chapter 6, the typical strategy of Japanese companies is better functionality at lower prices, and it leads them to lower ROS. I think it is true. However, Japanese companies hope to develop products and sell them to the targeted customers whom they focus on based on the U.S. management theory. When I had an interview with the CFO of a car manufacturer in 1994, he mentioned that 200,000 vehicles per one type of car per year in one factory needed producing at profitable cost. Actually it was so difficult that the product manager tried developing a car that expanded the targeted customer base. This means that too many specifications are incorporated into a car to respond to the needs of expanded targeted customers. The same goes for other industries.

It is so difficult for Japanese companies to overcome this problem, and nobody has found the solution. Under present circumstances described above, it is true that companies cannot earn enough profits. However, it is possible for them to be the companies that make a value proposition of "product leadership" and to avoid getting involved in price wars, as Apple does, or give up earning profits in Japanese markets and find new markets outside Japan. In these markets, Japanese companies should select targeted customers and develop products for only the targeted customers based on U.S. management theory.

Notes

1 See p. 63.
2 This formula is simplified version; the full formula is much more complicated. For further details, see Stewart (1990).
3 Actually there are many assumptions in the CAPM model. For example, all investors are rational and risk-averse, and trade without transaction costs and tax. For further details, see Glen (2012).
4 There are different opinions concerning whether short-term or long-term government bonds are acceptable. See Brealey et al. (2013) and Copeland et al. (2000).
5 Intuitively speaking, paying interest decreases net income decreases corporate tax. For example, interest of ¥10 million decreases net income by ¥10 million and thus decreases tax by ¥3.5 million in Japan. (The effective statutory tax rate was approximately 35 percent in Japan in 2014.)
6 For example, the percentage of foreign investors selling shares is 68 percent of total share sales at TSE and the percentage of foreign investors buying shares is 64 percent. See the website of the Japan Exchange Group: http://www.jpx.co.jp/markets/statistics-equities/investor-type/nlsgeu000001fv36-att/stock_val_1_160201.pdf.
7 This mail survey was conducted in 2009, and 68 companies (4 percent) responded. All question items were answered by a seven-point Likert scale (7: very important, 1: not important at all).
8 This mail survey was conducted from 2011 to 2012 and 187 companies (9.2 percent) answered this survey.
9 This mail survey was conducted in 2014 by the Life Insurance Association of Japan. 589 companies (54.8 percent) answered this survey.
10 In this survey, "Profit" includes gross margin, operating income, and so on.
11 In this survey, "Profit" includes gross margin, operating income, and so on. Also, this answer includes the growth rate of profit.
12 Keijo-Rieki is a profit concept in Japan. It is calculated as operating income plus finance income minus financial exchange. The Japanese word "Keijo-Rieki" means the profits by routine or ordinary businesses. This is a concept peculiar to Japan.
13 This includes ROE.
14 In this research, it is ROA.
15 In this research, it is ROA.
16 Its predecessor opened in 1878 but stopped mediating customer orders in 1945 and closed in 1947.
17 Keiretsu is a corporate group that has linked capital.
18 Capital ratio = Net Assets / Total Assets

References

Brealey, R.A., S.C. Meyers, and F. Allen (2013) *Principles of Corporate Finance*, 11th edition, New York, NY: McGraw-Hill/Irwin.

Copeland, T., T. Koller, and J. Murrin (2000) *Valuation*, 3rd edition, Hoboken, NJ: John Wiley & Sons.

Glen, A. (2012) *Corporate Financial Management*, 5th edition, Upper Saddle River, NJ: Pearson Education.

Kawano, K. (2014) The present situation and problems of the management accounting and the cost accounting of the Japanese companies, *The Study of Business and Industry, College of Commerce*, Nihon University, 30, 55–86. Written in Japanese.

The Life Insurance Association of Japan (2015) *The Approaches to Improve the Stock Value*, http://www.seiho.or.jp/info/news/2014/pdf/20150323_2.pdf.

Ministry of Economy, Trade and Industry (2014) *Ito Review of Competitiveness and Incentives for Sustainable Growth – Building Favorable Relationships between Companies and Investors*, http://www.meti.go.jp/english/press/2014/pdf/0806_04b.pdf.

Stewart, G.B. III (1990) *The Quest for Value*, New York, NY: Harper Business.

Yanagi, R. (2015) *The Financial Strategy by ROE Revolution*, Tokyo, Japan: Chuokeizai-sha Inc. Written in Japanese.

Yokota, E., T. Senoo, S. Takahashi, and Y. Goto (2013) A survey of performance management systems in Japanese companies, *Mita Business Review* (Keio University), 55(6), 67–87.

8 Management of advertising expenses in KAO

Key learning points

- What are marketing costs? How should companies manage them?
- Learn about the management of marketing costs in Kao.
- What is the "profit and advertising"? Why does Kao use it to manage marketing costs?

1. Introduction

It is difficult for most companies to manage marketing costs in selling, general, and administrative expenses (SGA). Managing marketing costs in selling expenses is the hardest task. Many companies spend a great amount of money for advertising but do not have an effective management tool to manage marketing costs, except a budgeting system.

In this chapter, I will introduce a way of managing marketing costs by using the example of advertising expenses in Kao. Kao is a chemical company, and it produces many famous household products such as laundry detergents (Attack), skin care products (Bioré), and shampoos (Asience). It is famous as one of the companies that introduced EVA® in Japan.[1] However, Kao has a distinctive way to manage advertising expenses other than the use of EVA®, and we should examine it.

2. Theory of management of marketing costs

1960s

In the 1960s there were some notable reports that were published by NAA.[2] This research related to management accounting for non-manufacturing functions, including:

NAA19 (1951) Assignment of Non-Manufacturing Costs for Managerial Decisions
NAA20 (1951) Assignment of Non-Manufacturing Costs for Products

NAA21 (1952) Assignment of Non-Manufacturing Costs to Territories and Other Segments
NAA25 (1954) Cost Control for Marketing Operations – General Consideration
NAA26 (1954) Cost Control for Marketing Operations – Order Getting
NAA27 (1954) Cost Control for Marketing Operations – Order Filling
NAA29 (1955) Accounting for Research and Development Costs

Nishizawa (1996) shows that there are some reasons why many research reports were published by NAA. One of the important reasons lies in the Robinson-Patman Act that was enacted in 1936. This is an Anti-Price Discrimination Act that prohibits price discrimination to get around competition. In other words, companies can sell the same products to customers at different prices due to different costs. When manufacturers make the same products, manufacturing costs become nearly equal. However, marketing costs may be different in each product or in each selling area. Thus, marketing costs were focused on in those days.[3]

Marketing costs are non-manufacturing costs in a broad sense (Nishizawa, 1996, p. 366). According to this interpretation, marketing costs include research and development costs. However, in this book R&D costs are excluded from marketing costs because R&D costs are essentially different from marketing costs.

Marketing costs are classified into order getting costs and order filling costs, as NAA25 and 26 indicate. Order getting costs include advertising expenses and sales promotion costs. Order filling costs include logistics costs. The latter are comparatively easy to control because they are as physical, repetitive, and typical as manufacturing costs. In contrast, the former are personal, non-repetitive, and unprogrammed. They are, therefore, much more difficult to manage than order filling costs. That is why there are few approaches to managing order getting costs aside from a budgeting system.

After 1990

Some research on the management of marketing costs (order getting costs) has recently been conducted in the management accounting area. Most management accounting research focusing on a market or customer is related to customer profitability (for example, Foster et al., 1996). Gupta and Zeithmal (2006) show that marketing activities influence customers' thinking, and customers' thinking influences customers' actions that eventuate in the financial performance in companies. This relation is shown in the European Customer Satisfaction Index (ECSI) developed by the ECSI Steering Committee (ECSI Technical Committee, 1998). In this model, this committee explains that four factors – image, customer expectations, perceived quality product characteristics, and service characteristics – are required to get customer retention. Thus appropriate activities including R&D, marketing, and manufacturing must be prepared for good performance.

We can find papers showing that financial performance depends on customer loyalty or customer actions. For example, BSCs draw the impact of customer satisfaction on financial performance. There are also some papers discussing the factors in the ECSI model.[4] In this model, image plays an important role in yielding customer satisfaction.[5]

Of course, marketing activities creating a good image for a product incur costs. Foster and Gupta (1994) discuss the relationship between marketing and cost management. Morgan et al. (2002) provides a contextual framework for marketing performance measurement systems. However, little progress has been made in the research into the management of advertising costs. Traditionally advertising expenses are managed by the budgeting system, and they are treated as policy costs. That is, a budget for advertising expenses is politically decided by top management based on the forecast of circumstances for the next fiscal year. Thus marketing managers must execute their budgets. Once economic conditions become severe, top management stop budget spending.

Kao has a distinctive management tool to control advertising expenses. It empowers brand managers to decide and control their advertising expenses. This system will be explained later.

Traditional method of managing marketing costs: budgeting

Traditionally, budgeting is the sole system to manage marketing costs, especially order getting costs. To manage these, companies may use two types of budgeting. One is policy cost budgeting and the other is zero-based budgeting.

Policy costs are strategically decided by top management. This type of cost includes advertising expenses and research and development costs. Companies usually measure the efficiency of costs. For example, they can measure the efficiency of manufacturing costs by calculating manufacturing costs per product or compare actual costs with standard costs. Companies can prepare the standard costs (or predetermined costs) per product. However, they cannot prepare these standard costs as to policy costs because the relationship between the costs and outputs (sales of products) is unclear and immeasurable. That is why top management collect information, and based on it they decide how much of a budget to prepare. Of course they do not always have good information or make great decisions. The budget for marketing often increases or decreases by some percent over the previous year, depending on the prospect for the future.

A new tool? Zero-based budgeting and activity-based budgeting

Zero-based budgeting (ZBB) was developed by Texas Instruments in the 1970s. ZBB is a budgeting system in which managers evaluate and select an action plan called "a decision package" with zero-based thinking. Zero-based thinking means that evaluation and selection of action plans are not mired in the past and are based on only the importance of these action plans to implement a

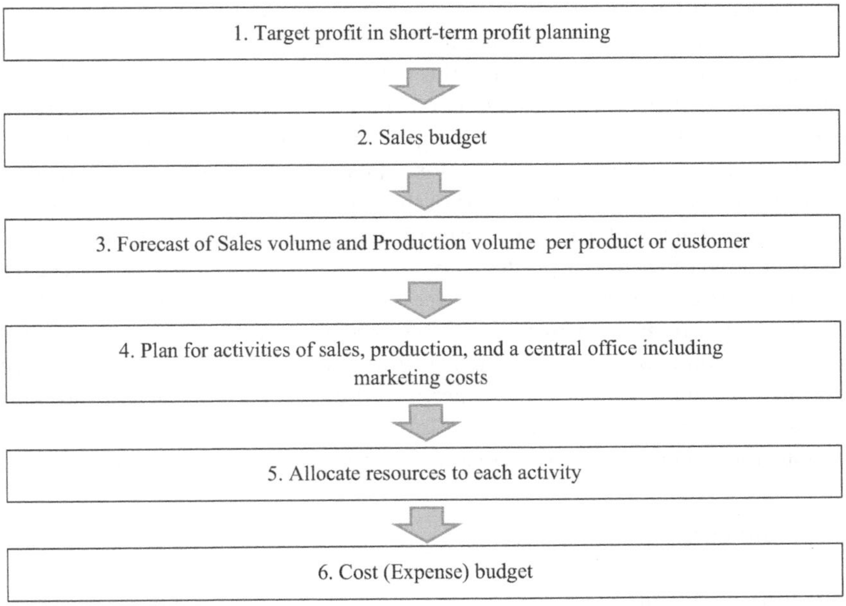

Figure 8.1 Flow of ABB
Adapted from (Shimizu, 2004, p. 175)

strategy. Zero-based budgeting did not become popular, because making and ranking decision packages were too troublesome a task.

After that, as is well known, activity-based costing (ABC) and activity-based management (ABM) were developed in the 1990s. Although I cannot explain the details and history of ABC and ABM because of space constraints, it is very clear that ABC and ABM are important theories in management accounting.[6]

Activity-based budgeting (ABB) is a budgeting system using the ABC concept. According to Brimson and Antos (1994, p. 267), ABB is "the process of planning and controlling the expected activities of the organization to derive a cost-effective budget that meets forecast workload and agreed strategic goals."

In the ABC structure, resources are consumed by activities, and the activities are consumed to make cost objects. In contrast, ABB has a process reverse to ABC. In fact, it starts with making a short-term profit plan, as shown in Figure 8.1. Next, companies prepare a sales budget. They forecast sales volume and production volume based on required sales (sales budget). To make and sell products and to support these functions, many activities must be prepared. All activities need resources, and resources should be allocated to them in a cost-effective and cost-efficient manner.

In this process, companies must not plan a cost budget in the way of reducing budgets compared with the previous year. Budgets must be planned as "zero-based."

Companies must input only resources necessary to attain target profit in a short-term profit plan independently of past costs. This is totally the same idea as ZBB.[7]

I think that this process of first planning actions and then allocating resources is highly efficient, and I believe that this is an ideal form for budgeting. Although there is no evidence that Japanese companies use ABB, managers say that they adopt this method into budget planning of direct manufacturing costs. However, the budget for marketing costs is more difficult to prepare by ABB than the budget for manufacturing costs. One of the reasons is that it is difficult to conduct cost-benefit analyses of marketing costs. In fact, manufacturing costs have a definite connection with particular products, but we cannot find a clear cost-benefit relationship between marketing costs and sales.[8] Thus there is no alternative but to decide desired budgets by managers. Now, who are managers? As discussed previously, marketing costs are set as "policy costs" and decided by top management. Top management cannot decide appropriate budgets because they do not know the details of each product and how much marketing costs it needs. For this reason, Kao empowers brand managers to make budgets for marketing costs.

3. The company outline

The history of Kao

Kao Corporation is one of the famous chemical companies in Japan. The predecessor of Kao Corporation – Nagase Corporation – was established by Tomiro Nagase in 1887. It was originally a notions store. He sold soap but it was of worse quality than soap made in foreign countries. He decided to produce good-quality soap by himself and started to sell it in 1890. At that time, it was a luxury and had a value of more than 10,000 yen in modern money. Then he started to build a factory and made face lotion, toothpaste, and chemical products as well as soap. Since then, Kao has been producing many products for daily needs. In 1989, Kao acquired Kanebo Cosmetics,[9] and now it is the second largest manufacturer in the Japanese cosmetics industry. Now Kao is a global company that has many consolidated subsidiaries in 17 countries.[10]

Kao has two businesses: consumer products and chemical. The consumer products business is sorted into three groups: beauty care, human health care, and fabric and home care. Products produced by each business are shown in Table 8.1.

Financial performance

Financial performance in the fiscal year 2014 and 2015 is shown in Table 8.2. Beauty care products have the largest net sales, but fabric and home care products have the largest operating income. Financial performance, net sales, and operating income continually increase.[11]

Kao is winning top share in some products in Japan. It competes with P&G and Unilever globally. Table 8.3 compares the financial performance of these three companies.

Table 8.1 The products in Kao

Consumer products business		
Beauty care business	Cosmetics	Counseling cosmetics, self-selection cosmetics
	Skin care products	Soaps, facial cleansers, body cleansers
	Hair care products	Shampoos, conditioners, hair styling agents, hair coloring agents
Human health care business	Food and beverage products	Beverage
	Sanitary products	Sanitary napkins, baby diapers
	Personal health products	Bath additives, oral care products, men's products
Fabric and home care business	Fabric care products	Laundry detergents, fabric treatments
	Home care products	Kitchen cleaning products, house cleaning products, paper cleaning products, commercial-use products
Chemical business		
Olea chemicals		Fatty alcohols, fatty amines, fatty acids, glycerin, commercial-use edible fats and oils
Performance chemicals		Surfactants, plastics additives, superplasticizers for concrete admixtures
Specialty chemicals		Toner and toner binder for copiers and printers, ink and colorants for inkjet printers, fragrances and aroma chemicals

Adapted from http://www.kao.com/jp/en/corp_info/business.html

Table 8.2 Financial performance

	Net sales		*Operating income*	
	Millions of U.S. dollars		*Millions of U.S. dollars*	
	2015	*2014*	*2015*	*2014*
Beauty care	5,044.3	4,896.7	244.2	236.0
Human health care	2,330.2	1,992.8	295.1	181.6
Fabric and home care	2,775.9	2,693.7	574.7	506.0
Consumer products total	10,150.5	9.583.2	1,114.0	923.6
Chemical	2,394.4	2,390.8	250.0	183.1
Total	12,544.9	11,974.0	1,363.9	1,106.7
Reconciliations	(327.8)	(338.7)	0.5	(0.5)
Consolidated	12,217.1	11,635.3	1,364.5	1,106.3

Adapted from http://www.kao.com/jp/en/corp_ir/imgs/results_fy2015_all.pdf

Table 8.3 Kao, P&G, and Unilever

		2015	*2014*
Kao	Net sales	12,217	11,636
($ million)	Operating income	1,365	1,106
P&G	Sales	76,279	80,510
($ million)	Operating income	11,790	14,740
Unilever	Turnover	53,272	48,436
(€ million)	Operating profit	7,515	7,980

Adapted from http://www.kao.com/jp/en/corp_ir/imgs/results_fy2015_all.pdfhttp://www.pginvestor.com/Financial-Highlights/Index?KeyGenPage=209707https://www.unilever.com/Images/annual_report_and_accounts_ar15_tcm244-478426_en.pdf

The Kao Way

The Kao Way is the corporate philosophy of Kao. It was declared in 2004 as a revision of the earlier corporate philosophy. It is the foundation of all the activities in the Kao group. It has a quadruplex structure, as shown in Figure 8.2.

Kao's mission is to satisfy and enrich the lives of people. It makes employees' growth align with Kao's development, as well as gives employees a coherent message about operation and management.

There are some characteristic Japanese words in the Kao Way. "Yoki-Monozukuri" is exactly a vital component to it, and means "a strong commitment by all members to provide products and brands of excellent value for consumer satisfaction" (http://www. kao.com/jp/en/corp_about/kaoway_02.html).[12] This type of corporate philosophy is often adopted by Japanese companies. Companies (and employees) work to make people who use their products comfortable.

In the Kao principles you can see "Genba-ism." *Gemba* means generally a job site or a factory floor. In the Kao Way, Gemba-ism is defined as "the importance of observing things on-site, in the actual location and environment, both internally and externally, in order to maximize our understanding of the business and optimize our performance" (http://www.kao.com/jp/en/corp_about/kaoway_03.html). Externally, Kao considers that customers' experiences are critical. Thus it requires that all employees should understand consumers by visiting them. Internally, it requires that all employees should cooperate to put out good products, and considers that the ideas from the internal Gemba are very important. In Japan, it is often said that Gemba is smart (employees working at the front line are so smart). Front-line employees are empowered to devise their work in a factory or sales floor. They are always exploring the possibilities for improvement on an autonomous basis. It is said that this behavior is one of the sources of the competitive advantage in Japanese companies. The

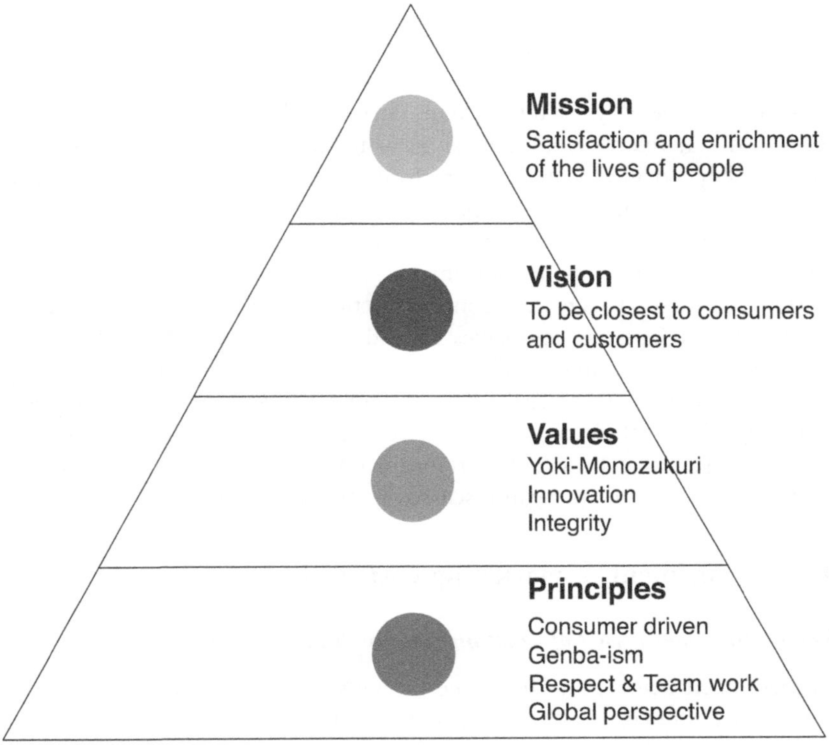

Figure 8.2 The Kao way

Source: http://www.kao.com/group/en/group/kaoway.html

scope of employees' authority is explicit in some cases and implicit in other cases in Japan. In many countries, it must be clearly stated (explicit), because if not, employees do not understand an upper limit to what they can do. This characteristic may be derived from the national culture in Japan.

High-context communication

Mayer (2015) developed an eight-scale[13] culture model. In this model, "each of the eight scales represents one key area that managers must be aware of, showing how cultures vary along a spectrum from one extreme to its opposite" (Mayer, 2015, p. 15). In this model, national culture is classified into two types: high-context and low- context (Mayer, 2015, p. 39).

Low-context: Good communication is precise, simple, and clear. Messages are expressed and understood at face value. Repetition is appreciated if it helps clarify the communication.

High-context: Good communication is sophisticated, nuanced, and layered. Messages are both spoken and read between the lines. Messages are often implied but not plainly expressed.

According to the Mayer Culture Map, Japan has the highest context culture in the world. Therefore, employees know what and how to do their jobs, even though they do not receive orders from their bosses explicitly. Employees understand from their bosses' expression or atmosphere what their bosses (and top management) expect them to do. Thus, "vertical" interactive controls potentially exist in Japanese companies.

Many Japanese management control practices are based on this high-context culture. When Japanese companies expand overseas (especially to low-context countries), there is often conflict between local and overseas employees. To operate companies effectively, it is important for both Japanese employees and employees from other countries to understand their cultural differences. This aspect of Japanese culture is important for understanding the cases of management control systems in Japan discussed in the following sections.

4. Management of marketing costs in Kao

The management unit of consumer products business in Kao

As mentioned before, Kao has three businesses in its consumer products line: beauty care, human health care, and fabric and home care. Each business is under the control of a manager of this business unit. Under the business manager, there are some product groups, and they are controlled by their business managers. For example, as shown in Table 8.1, the beauty care business has three sub-categories: cosmetics, skin care products, and hair care products. And each subcategory has some product groups. For example, there are soaps, facial cleansers, and body cleansers in skin care products, as shown in Table 8.4. Finally, each product group has some brands. For example, the facial cleanser has the brand "Bioré" and "Men's Bioré." Each brand has some products. Bioré has various kinds of products – for example, baking soda pore cleanser, baking soda cleansing scrub, self-heating one minute mask, acne clearing scrub, and deep cleansing pore strips. Basically, the management unit is a brand. Brand managers make decisions on management of their products.

Income statement by brand in Kao

Brand managers make plans to produce and sell their products and implement these plans. To do that, they use the income statement in the form of direct costing. Contribution margin is sales minus variable costs. Contribution margin minus fixed costs is operating income. Generally variable costs include manufacturing and selling (marketing) costs, and fixed costs include manufacturing, selling, general, and administrative costs.

Table 8.4 Domain, product group, and main brands in the beauty care business

Subcategory	*Product group*	*Main brands*
Cosmetics	Counseling cosmetics self-selection cosmetics	Sofina Kanebo
Skin care products	Soaps facial cleansers body cleansers	Bioré, Men's Bioré, Jergens
Hair care products	Shampoos Conditioners hair styling agents hair coloring agents	Asience, Segreta, Molton Brown, John Frida, Goldwell

Adapted from websites of Kao

Table 8.5 Income statement by brand

Income statement by brand	
Sales	XXX
Variable costs	
Manufacturing	XXX
Selling	XXX
Contribution margin	XXX
Fixed costs	
Manufacturing	XXX
Selling and general administrative	XXX
Profit and advertising	XXX
Marketing costs	XXX
Operating income	XXX

(From the interview with Yoshinori Fujita, the manager of KAO, on January 10, 2013)

The income statement by brand is different from the general direct costing income statement. Table 8.5 shows that variable costs include manufacturing costs and fixed costs include manufacturing and selling and general administrative costs, but neither of these include "marketing costs," which are normally part of selling costs. Here, marketing costs are advertising expenses and sales promotion costs that are getting order costs. Marketing costs are usually classified as fixed costs. Kao subtracts "marketing costs" from fixed costs to control marketing costs. Order filling costs such as logistics costs are included in variable and fixed costs.

Management by income statement

Brand managers work to manage their brand in terms of the selling of products. They do not have any authority to manufacture nor research and develop. They focus on making an appropriate operating income by controlling "profit and advertising."

The target of each brand manager is profit and advertising (P&A) as well as sales budget. The specific target of P&A in Kao is 30 percent of sales. That is, sales budget is a measure of volume, and P&A is a measure of the quality of profit. A breakdown of targeted P&A is that 1/3 is profits, 1/3 is taxes, and 1/3 is marketing costs. When P&A exceeds 30 percent of sales, brand managers can invest (or expense) this excess amount in their brand.

In budgeting, brand managers decide a marketing cost budget based on the forecast of sales. Of course, brand managers always work together with manufacturing and R&D managers because they do not have any authority to manufacture nor research and develop. If brand managers have some trouble making targeted profits, they may consult with manufacturing managers. If they find their products uncompetitive, they may consult with R&D managers about the improvement of products.

When making a plan, brand managers always try to earn P&A that reaches 30 percent of sales. What action will they take when the forecast gets worse than that? Let us look at three types of brand managers' way of thinking.

(1) An increase in a market share

Brand managers are responsible for attaining the sales budget as well as the market share of each product. When the market is stable, the market share target is almost the same as the sales target. However, if the market of a product is growing more than a brand manager's forecast, it is not enough that a manager just attains the sales budget.

When brand managers find a market share of a product lower than expected, they place spot advertising within the budget limit. They know how much they should spend on advertisements on an empirical basis to recover a market share under the competitive situation. They also consult with an advertising manager about the selection of advertising media with the maximum effect and efficiency.

When brand managers attribute a decrease in a market share to the quality of products, they consult with managers in the manufacturing department about how to resolve this problem, instead of advertising.

(2) A decrease in costs

Brand managers should consider whether they can cut variable and fixed costs without decreasing sales. They have their brand budgeted income statements that show the cost structure of products. They understand how much they should carry out cost reduction and which cost item they should reduce.

(3) *An introduction of a new product*

When introducing a new product, brand managers set the targets of market share and sales. Next they review the costs with a R&D manager if they cannot earn targeted P&A. Of course, the target may be loosened for a little while after a new product is launched. In short, brand managers work to attain targeted P&A and are empowered to do so.

5. Discussions

As explained in Chapter 2, MSCs are a system to implement strategies, and I make use of the concept of Merchant and Van der Stede (2012), plus an organization in this book (see Figure 2.1). In Figure 2.1, management accounting tools are equal to result controls. I would like to explain the P&A system in Kao.

Kao uses the direct costing system to calculate P&A. It sets a brand team as a management unit to control P&A. Brand managers are empowered to manage their units, and they first plan sales and costs (except marketing costs). They must spend marketing costs on promoting the sale of their products. They always review the budget in this system and compare it with the forecast. Thus they can know what to do (and how much they should spend on advertising) to earn the required (budgeted) operating income through this system.

This system is not tightly linked with the bonus system. The bonus system in Japan uses a kind of holistic approach. When a company earns a big profit, all employees share it. Some products are very competitive and others are not. Brand managers assigned to competitive brands try to get more profits, and ones assigned to uncompetitive brands try to reduce losses and to make them profitable ultimately. Both of them contribute to an increase in company profits. However, the performance of brand managers influences their promotion. They are evaluated in the light of an attainment level of their profit budget, targeted

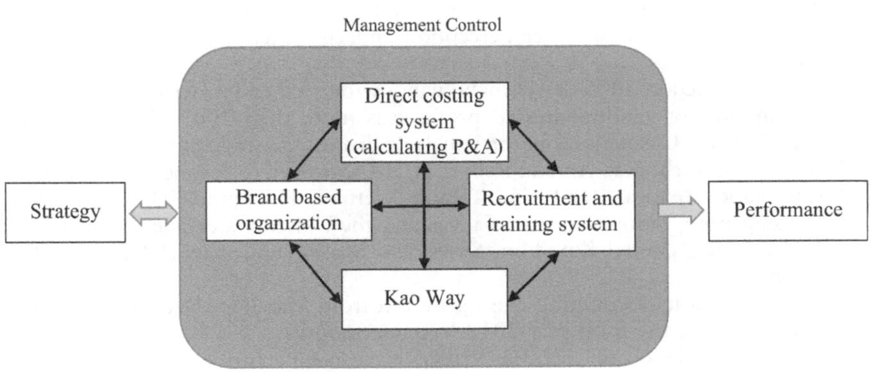

Figure 8.3 Strategic implementing system in Kao

market share, and actual profits compared with the previous year. The incentive system in Japan is based on a long-term perspective.

Personnel and action control is based on the Kao Way. This is the corporate philosophy and the guidelines for employees' actions. After recruitment, employees are trained to gain skills, and to understand and absorb the Kao Way.[14] Kao holds a workshop on the Kao Way at each section from top management to the front line. In this workshop, employees read the Kao Way in turn and discuss what all the contents mean. They also think about the relationship between values/principles and employees' daily work. Managers are engaged in this workshop and explain the Kao Way based on their experiences.

The Kao Way reflects the founder's and top management's thinking. It grows the culture focusing on "Yoki-Monozukuri" and "Genba-ism," and employees always regard the Kao Way as the center of their activities.

Notes

1 As of February 2015, Kao still calculates EVA®, but it is not controlled anymore.
2 NAA is the abbreviated name for National Association of Accountants and it is the predecessor of the Institute of Management Accountants (IMA). It is an organization for professional management accountants with over 70,000 members throughout the world. For further information, see http://www.imanet.org.
3 IMA published a new series of standards of management accounting (SMA), but there are no SMAs related to the management of marketing costs.
4 See Ciavolino and Dahlgaard (2007) and Ferreira et al. (2010).
5 Kristensen et al. (2002) conducted research on the introduction of ECSI theory into Post Office in Denmark and found that "image" had the biggest impact on customer loyalty.
6 Some origins of ABC are introduced. See (Cooper and Kaplan, 1988) and (Johnson, 1992). For details of ABM, see Kaplan and Cooper (1998).
7 Kaplan and Cooper (1998, p. 302) showed that if the concept had not become discredited by poor theory and application in the Carter administration, they could refer to activity-based budgeting as zero-based budgeting. ABB and ZBB are essentially the same thing.
8 There are many studies on the relationship between marketing costs and marketing effects such as customer perception and customer behaviors in marketing areas.
9 It was revealed in 2006 that Kanebo window-dressed its financial statement, and the amount of window-dressed profits was more than 200 billion yen. After that, Kanebo Cosmetics, one of Kanebo's divisions, was acquired by Kao.
10 According to the Kao Annual Report in 2014, written in Japanese, consolidated subsidiaries are located in China, Taiwan, Vietnam, Philippines, Thailand, Malaysia, Singapore, Indonesia, Australia, Canada, the United States, Mexico, Germany, Holland, the United Kingdom, Swiss, and Spain. (Kao Annual Report, 2015, p. 76)
11 Kao changed its accounting closing month from March to December in 2012. Consequently, the fiscal year 2012 has nine months.
12 A literal translation of *Yoki-Monozukuri* is to manufacture good products.
13 This includes communicating (low-context versus high-context), evaluating (direct negative feedback versus indirect negative feedback), persuading (principles-first

versus applications-first), leading (egalitarian versus hierarchical), deciding (consensual versus top-down), trusting (task-based versus relationship-based), disagreeing (confrontational versus avoid confrontation), and scheduling (linear-time versus flexible-time).

14 The contents in this paragraph are based on the interview with Shunichi Nakagawa, the director of Kao at that time (http://www.nikkeibp.co.jp/article/hco/20111221/294493/?P=1).

References

Brimson, J. and J. Antos (1994) *Activity-based Management: For Service Industries, Government Entities, and Nonprofit Organizations*, New York, NY: John Wiley & Sons.

Ciavolino, E. and J. Dahlgaard (2007) ECSI – customer satisfaction modelling and analysis: A case study, *Total Quality Management*, 18(5), 545–554.

Cooper, R. and R.S. Kaplan (1988) Measure costs right: Make the right decisions, *Harvard Business Review*, 66(5), 96–103.

ECSI Technical Committee (1998) *European Customer Satisfaction Index: Foundation and Structure for Harmonized National Pilot Projects*, ECSI Steering Committee.

Ferreira, I., J. Cabral, and P. Saraiva (2010) An integrated framework based on the ECSI approach to link mould customers' satisfaction and product design, *Total Quality Management*, 21(12), 1383–1401.

Foster, G. and M. Gupta (1994) Marketing, cost management and management accounting, *Journal of Management Accounting Research*, 6, 43–77.

Foster, G., M. Gupta, and L. Sjoblom (1996) Customer profitability analysis: Challenge and new directions, *Journal of Cost Management*, 10(1), 5–7.

Gupta, S. and V. Zeithmal (2006), Customer metrics and their impact on financial performance, *Marketing Science*, 25(6), 718–739.

Johnson, H.T. (1992) *Relevance Regained: From Top-Down Control to Bottom-Up Empowerment*, New York, NY: Free Press.

Kao Corporation, *Annual Report 2014*, http://www.kao.com/jp/en/corp_ir/imgs/reports_fy2014e_all.pdf.

Kaplan, R.S. and R. Cooper (1998) *Cost and Effect: Using Integrated Cost Systems to Drive Profitability and Performance*, Boston, MA: Harvard Business School Press.

Kristensen, K., A. Martensen, and L. Grønholdt (2002) Customer satisfaction and business performance, in Neely, A. (ed.) *Business Performance Measurement: Theory and Practice*, Chapter 17, Cambridge, UK: Cambridge University Press, pp. 279–294.

Mayer, E. (2015) *The Culture Map: Decoding How People Think, Lead, and Get Things Done across Cultures: International edition*, New York, NY: PublicAffairs.

Morgan, N.A., B.H. Clark, and R. Gooner (2002) Marketing productivity, marketing audits, and systems for marketing performance assessment: Integrating multiple perspectives, *Journal of Business Research*, 55, 363–375.

Nishizawa, O. (1996) *Managerial Accounting for Management*, Tokyo, Japan: Chuokeizai-sha Inc. Written in Japanese.

Shimizu, T. (2004) The budgeting innovation in the short-term strategic management system, in Shimizu, T. (ed.) *The Strategic Management System: The Balanced Scorecard for Companies and Nonprofit Organizations*, Chapter 7, Tokyo, Japan: Chuokeizai-sha Inc. pp. 159–184. Written in Japanese.

9 Transfer pricing in Mitsubishi Electric

Key learning points

- What is transfer pricing?
- Learn there are some transfer prices.
- What are the objectives of transfer pricing?
- What is dual pricing, and why does Mitsubishi electric use it?

1. Introduction

Transfer pricing is one of the methods in management control systems. Transfer pricing is a system in which a company's subunit sets the internal price (the transfer price) to provide its products or services to another subunit in the same company. There are many subunits that work in collaboration in decentralized companies. The more closely they collaborate with each other, the more occasions they have to transfer products and services.

As shown in Chapter 5, there are two types of decentralized organization: vertical (the functional system) and horizontal (the division system). There are basically less transactions between subunits in the division system than those in the functional system. That is because each division is independent and has all functions of operations and management. In contrast, there are close relationships between divisions in the functional system, such as manufacturing and sales divisions, and assembling and parts divisions.

Each division has significant authority to make a decisions on selling products and buying parts and materials in a decentralized organization. That is, there are independent sellers and buyers in one company. A company sets its division as a profit center or an investment center. Therefore, division managers try to maximize their financial performance. In addition, they work together to maximize not only profits of their divisions but also those of the whole company. Thus, transfer pricing has two objectives. One is performance measurement of divisions, and the other is goal congruence. These two objectives often cause a trade-off problem because managers improve their own performance by sacrificing other divisions' or the whole company's performance.

In this chapter, I will explain some transfer prices and introduce the dual pricing in Mitsubishi Electric. Textbooks deal with dual pricing in the transfer pricing system but often say that there are few companies using dual pricing because it has some major problems. Then why does Mitsubishi Electric use dual pricing?

2. Theory of transfer pricing

Research on transfer pricing

Research on transfer pricing has been widely conducted since the 1950s. There are two types of studies about transfer pricing. One is to list traditional transfer prices and to relate certain management circumstances to one of them. The other is to consider the economic development of traditional transfer prices. Some examples of the former studies are Anthony et al. (1989), Benk and Edwards (1980), Eccles (1985), and Kaplan (1988). Eccles (1985) describes two corporate strategies – vertical combination and diversification – and how companies should select a transfer price with the combination of these strategies and their depth. A representative example of the latter studies is Ronen and McKinney (1970). They calculate the optimal transfer price by using mathematical economics. Although their models have restrictions with so many assumptions, after that, Dejong and et al. (1989) and Ronen and Balachandran (1988) extend their study. This type of study is published a lot now, but I do not deal with their studies in this book because they do not seem to be practical.

International transfer pricing is very important from a perspective of international taxation. However, this topic is not treated in this book because it relates to the transfer pricing regulations in various countries.

Traditional classification of transfer prices

Transfer prices are classified into three categories, basically depending on whether or not there is a market of transferred goods and services. They are as follows:

1 Market-based transfer prices
   a Market-based price
   b Market-based price minus some avoidable costs incurred by internal transactions
2 Cost-based transfer prices
   A Cost basis
      - Full cost basis
      - Variable cost basis
   B Cost plus profit basis
      - Full cost plus profit basis
      - Variable cost plus profit basis

3 Other transfer prices
 A Negotiated pricing
 B Dual pricing

Market-based transfer prices

A. MARKET-BASED PRICE

When division managers find the price of transferred goods in the open market, they can select market-based transfer prices as a transfer price. Market-based transfer prices are the most objective price if there are many buyers and sellers and they are price takers. In this case, a company's subunit has the authority to buy or sell goods or services to or from the inside or outside of the company.

Let us suppose that company A is a chemical manufacturer and has two divisions. Division A makes product X, and division B makes product Y by processing product X. Product X and Y are traded in the market, and the market price of product X is 5,000 yen per kilogram and that of product Y is 10,000 yen per kilogram. The manufacturing costs per kilogram of product X and product Y are shown in Table 9.1. The volume of transferred product X is 1,000 kilograms.

In this case, if division A is required by division B to sell product X for less than 5,000 yen, division A rejects division B's demands because it can sell product X for 5,000 yen in the market. Also, if division A proposes selling division B product X for more than 5,000 yen, division B should buy product X from an outside supplier. Thus the market price of product X, 5,000 yen, is the most appropriate transfer price. When divisions use market-based transfer prices, their income statements are shown in Table 9.2.

Table 9.1 Manufacturing costs of products X and Y (yen)

	Product X	*Product Y*
Direct material costs[1]	1,500	Transfer price
Direct labor costs[2]	1,000	1,000
Overhead costs[3]	1,000	2,000
Total	3,500	

Table 9.2 Income statements (produced by using market-based transfer prices)

	Division A	*Division B*	*Consolidated*
Sales	5,000,000	10,000,000	10,000,000
Direct material costs	1,500,000	5,000,000	1,500,000
Direct labor costs	1,000,000	1,000,000	2,000,000
Overhead costs	1,000,000	2,000,000	3,000,000
Gross margin	1,500,000	2,000,000	3,500,000

B. MARKET-BASED PRICE MINUS SOME AVOIDABLE COSTS INCURRED BY INTERNAL TRANSACTIONS

Transfer transactions are carried out between two divisions in a company. Differing from transactions between companies, internal transactions do not need some types of cost such as advertising expenses or physical distribution costs. If it is possible for a company to measure these costs, the company can deduct these costs from the market price.

Cost-based transfer prices

A. COST BASIS

If there is no market for transferred products, how should a company calculate transfer prices? In this case, companies may select cost-based transfer prices. There are two types of cost-based transfer price: a cost basis and a cost plus profit basis.

On a cost basis, intermediate products are transferred at manufacturing full costs or variable costs. When this company uses a full cost basis, division A transfers product X for 3,500 yen. Income statements of both divisions are shown in Table 9.3. In this case, the operating income of division A is zero. Although these divisions are profit centers or investment centers, a cost basis transfer price is useless because division A has no profit and the manager of division A must be dissatisfied with this situation. Thus, if there is no market for transferred products, a cost plus profit basis should be used in the division systems.

Cost basis transfer prices may be used for the most appropriate decision making for the whole company. Differing from the case in Table 9.3, when each division is independent, transferred products are small in quantity, and division A has excess capacity, variable cost basis transfer prices are useful for accomplishing two objectives.

Let us suppose that division A and B make different products and sell them to different customers. Division B considers making new products. It seeks suppliers of an electronic substrate. It finds some candidates, and one of them is division A. Variable costs per substrate are 1,900 yen, and fixed costs per substrate are 1,600 yen. Division A makes substrates without any capacity investment. The lowest price offered by an outside supplier is 3,000 yen.

Table 9.3 Income statements (produced by using cost basis transfer prices)

	Division A	*Division B*	*Consolidated*
Sales	3,500,000	10,000,000	10,000,000
Direct material costs	1,500,000	3,500,000	1,500,000
Direct labor costs	1,000,000	1,000,000	2,000,000
Overhead costs	1,000,000	2,000,000	3,000,000
Gross margin	0	3,500,000	3,500,000

If division A proposes selling division B substrates at a full cost of 3,500 yen, division B would buy them from this supplier. However, this decision is not best for this company. Division A does not incur any additional fixed costs, even though it makes substrates because it has excess capacity. The optimum decision for the whole company is that division A uses its capacity and division B earns maximum profits. To do that, division A should transfer a substrate at a variable cost to division B.

When companies apply a cost basis to a transfer price, they must use standard costs, not actual costs, because actual costs may include costs incurred by production inefficiency in a seller (division A).

B. COST PLUS PROFIT BASIS

As explained previously, a cost basis transfer price is not appropriate for the division system because a profit center and an investment center in the division system are basically evaluated by their profits. Thus, divisions should use a cost plus profit basis transfer price. For example, when there is no market nor supplier for product X – that is, no market price – division A may transfer product X at the full cost plus 20 percent of full cost (see Table 9.4). To decide how much markup should be (in this case, 20 percent of full cost), two divisions talk with each other, or the central office may intermediate between two divisions.

Other transfer prices

A. NEGOTIATED PRICING

When there is no market for transferred products, a company may use a cost basis price. However, as stated previously, when divisions use a cost plus profit basis transfer price, appropriate markup is determined by negotiation between a seller, division A, and a buyer, division B. Because both divisions try to make profits, the transfer price is set between 3,500 yen and 5,000 yen. The

Table 9.4 Income statements (produced by using cost plus profit basis)

	Division A	*Division B*	*Consolidated*
Sales	4,200,000	10,000,000	10,000,000
Direct material costs	1,500,000	4,200,000	1,500,000
Direct labor costs	1,000,000	1,000,000	2,000,000
Overhead costs	1,000,000	2,000,000	3,000,000
Gross margin	700,000	2,800,000	3,500,000

managers of division A and B negotiate for a contract under favorable conditions for them. This is a kind of essence of business, and a buyer and a seller have the authority to negotiate the transfer price under autonomous conditions. However, this type of transfer price leads division managers to sub-optimize decisions.

B. DUAL PRICING

It is often said that no transfer prices described previously achieve two objectives of transfer pricing (goal congruence and performance measurement). This is not a problem in the case in which transactions between two divisions are not frequent and the percentage of transaction value between divisions to total transactions is small. As the volume of transactions grows, every transfer price often leads division managers to make more sub-optimized actions; that is to say, they may sacrifice a company's profits on the altar of their profits. This is because when divisions use market-based transfer prices, all profits of an internal transaction are attributed to a selling division, and when they use cost basis transfer prices, all profits are attributed to a buying division. If divisions are set as profit centers, one of them must be dissatisfied with this situation where the division has no profit. In this case, they start to negotiate over the transfer of products in favor of themselves.

I take an example of the transaction between a manufacturing division and a sales division (as shown in Chapter 5, many Japanese companies use a functional system). A manufacturing division makes product S, and all of the manufactured products are transferred to a sales division. Total manufacturing costs of each product S are 2,000 yen, and the number of transferred units is 1,000. This company estimates the price of product S is 3,000 yen by a sales division. The result of the use of market-based prices is shown on the left side and that of the use of cost basis prices is on the right side of Table 9.5.

Table 9.5 Income statements: market-based prices vs. cost basis prices

	Income statement by the use of market-based prices		*Income statement by the use of cost basis prices*	
	M	*S*	*M*	*S*
Sales	3,000,000	3,000,000	2,000,000	3,000,000
Manufacturing costs	2,000,000	—	2,000,000	—
Purchase amount	—	3,000,000	—	2,000,000
Sales costs	—	200,000	—	200,000
Operating profit	1,000,000	–200,000	0	800,000

Table 9.6 Income statements (dual pricing)

	M	*S*	*Consolidated*
Sales	3,000,000	3,000,000	3,000,000
Manufacturing costs	2,000,000	—	2,000,000
Purchase amount	—	2,000,000	—
Sales costs	—	200,000	200,000
Operating profit	1,000,000	800,000	800,000

In the real world, when both divisions are set as a profit center or an investment center, they spend much time negotiating for an advantageous transfer price. It wastes their valuable time because the total operating profit never changes even if a company uses any transfer price.

There are two ways to avoid this problem. One is that a sales division charges a manufacturing division a commission on sales of product S. A manufacturing division transfers product S at the market-based price to a sales division. A sales division makes efforts to sell products to customers and receives sales commissions from a manufacturing division. This method is sometimes used by Japanese companies. I will show you a detailed case of Kyocera in Chapter 11. The other is to use dual pricing, where selling divisions sell their products to buying divisions at the market price and buying divisions receive them at full costs.

Using the case described previously, income statements of both divisions are shown in Table 9.6.

By using dual pricing, a company can attain both objectives of performance measurement and goal congruence. However, the demerit of dual pricing may mislead divisions. Although the total (consolidated) profits are 800,000 yen, a manufacturing division has a profit of 1,000,000 yen and a sales division has a profit of 800,000 yen. That is, operating profit is double counted. Thus, it is generally said "dual pricing is not widely used in practice" (Horngren et al., 2012, p. 789). Mitsubishi Electric uses the dual pricing system for the objectives that manufacturing and sales divisions cooperate on to maximize corporate profits.

3. The company outline

The history of Mitsubishi Electric

Mitsubishi Electric (ME) is one of the largest electric manufacturers and a member of the Mitsubishi group. The predecessor of ME was founded by Yataro Iwasaki, who is a famous businessperson in Japan because he contributed to the modernization of Japan. He started a marine transportation and a trade company in the19th century. In 1917, he established a ship builder, and ME was spun off from it in 1921. Now it has 10 business groups, and some examples of divisions as of 2016 are shown in Table 9.7.

The organization form of ME is the division system. The largest category is the "group," with 14 groups total. Four out of 14 groups are in charge of

Table 9.7 List of groups in ME

Business groups	*Examples of departments and divisions*
Information systems and network service group	Planning and administration
	Information systems and network service
Public utility systems group	Planning and administration
	Transportation systems
	Plant engineering and construction
	Kobe Works, Itami Works, Nagasaki Works
Energy and industrial systems group	Planning and administration
	Transmission and distribution systems marketing
	Power and energy systems marketing
	Energy systems center, transmission and distribution systems center, power distribution systems center
Building systems group	Planning and administration
	Total security systems
	Building systems field operation
	Inazawa Works
Electronic systems group	Planning and administration
	Defense systems
	Space systems, IT space solutions
	Kamakura Works, Communication systems center
Communication systems group	Planning and administration
	Telecommunication systems sales and marketing
	Communication network center
Living environment and digital media equipment group	Planning and administration
	Eco-facility systems marketing
	Air-conditioning and refrigeration systems
	Home appliances and digital media equipment
	Nakatsugawa Works, Air-Conditioning and Refrigeration Systems Works, Shizuoka Works, Kyoto Works, Gunma Works
Factory automation systems group	Planning and administration
	Industrial products marketing
	Industrial automation marketing
	Nagoya Works, Fukuyama Works
Automotive equipment group	Planning and administration
	Automotive equipment marketing
	Himeji Works, Sanda Works
Semiconductor and device group	Planning and administration
	Semiconductor and device marketing
	Power Device Works, High Frequency and Optical Device Works

http://www.mitsubishielectric.com/company/about/organization/org/index.html

support functions of the whole company, such as marketing, strategic planning, productivity management, and R&D. Ten groups in Table 9.7 are "divisions." Each division has some departments, including sales force, factories ("works" in Table 9.7), and some support departments.

Financial performance

Financial performance in the fiscal year 2014 and 2015 is shown in Table 9.8.

ME competes with two general electronic manufacturers, Hitachi and Toshiba. Table 9.9 shows the outline of these three companies' financial performance.

Table 9.8 Financial performance

	Net sales		*Operating income*	
	Millions of yen		*Millions of yen*	
	2015	*2014*	*2015*	*2014*
Energy and electric systems	1,228,958	1,180,093	72,448	76,324
Industrial automation systems	1,282,749	1,098,796	145,982	98,079
Information and communication systems	559,521	548,282	18,934	5,529
Electric devices	238,402	194,658	30,163	10,050
Home appliances	944,830	944,351	54,296	52,878
Others	740,517	676,034	23,742	19,801
Subtotal	4,994,977	4,642,214	345,565	262,661
Eliminations and other	(671,936)	(587,855)	(27,961)	(27,489)
Total	4,323,041	4,054,359	317,604	235,172

Adapted from http://www.mitsubishielectric.com/company/ir/library/results/pdf/fy2015_2/1.pdf (p. 10)

Table 9.9 ME, Hitachi, and Toshiba

		2015	*2014*
ME	Net sales	4,323.0	4,054.4
(¥ billion)	Operating income	317.6	235.2
Hitachi	Sales	9,774.9	9,666.4
(¥ billion)	Operating income	641.3	604.7
Toshiba	Sales	6,655.9	6,489.7
(¥ billion)	Operating profit	170.4	257.1

Adapted from http://www.mitsubishielectric.com/company/ir/library/results/pdf/fy2015_4/3.pdf
http://www.hitachi.com/IR-e/financial/pl/index.html
http://www.toshiba.co.jp/about/ir/en/finance/pl.htm

Table 9.10 Corporate mission and seven guiding principles

Corporate mission

The Mitsubishi Electric Group will continually improve its technologies and services by applying creativity to all aspects of its business. By doing so, we enhance the quality of life in our society. To this end, all members of the group will pursue the following seven guiding principles.

Seven guiding principles

1 Trust: Establish relationships with society, customers, shareholders, employees, and business partners based on strong mutual trust and respect.

2 Quality: Provide the best products and services with unsurpassed quality.

3 Technology: Pioneer new markets by promoting research and development, and fostering technological innovation.

4 Citizenship: As a global player, contribute to the development of communities and society as a whole.

5 Ethics and compliance: In all endeavors, conduct ourselves in compliance with applicable laws and high ethical standards.

6 Environment: Respect nature, and strive to protect and improve the global environment.

7 Growth: Ensure fair earnings to build a foundation for future growth.

http://www.mitsubishielectric.com/company/about/mission/index.html

Corporate mission

ME has a corporate mission and seven guiding principles (see Table 9.10) to guide employees to do things in the right way.

ME involves a training meeting so that the corporate mission and seven guiding principles penetrate new recruits, but no special session and approach except this meeting are seen.

4. Dual transfer pricing system in ME

As explained in Section 2, companies may use dual pricing to attain goal of both congruence and performance measurement when two divisions are closely related. The following is a case of dual pricing at ME. Take notice that this case is simplified, and the practice at ME is much more complex.

In ME, manufacturing departments are called works[4] and sales departments are called divisions.[5] For example, in the Living Environment and Digital Media Equipment Group, Shizuoka Works makes refrigerators and air conditioners and transfers them to the Air-Conditioning and Refrigeration System Division. Thus, the dual transfer pricing system is used for the transfer of products from a manufacturing department to a selling department in the division, not for the transfer between two divisions.

Works basically make products and transfer them to divisions.[6] The matrix income statement that ME uses is shown in Figure 9.1. A works identifies "cost

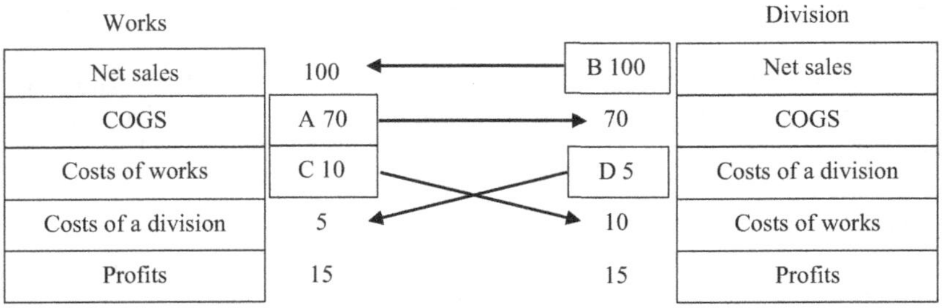

Figure 9.1 The matrix income statement

of goods sold" (COGS) of products and transfers them to a division on a full cost basis (A). When a division sells these products at a price of \$100 to a customer, a division identifies the \$100 and transfers this information to the works, and the works also identifies sales of \$100 (B). In addition, works and divisions share their cost information with each other. When the works pays its costs to operate it (C), the works tells its costs to a division, and when a division pays its costs, it tells them to the works (D). As a result, this matrix shows revenues and all of the manufacturing, selling and administrative costs for products. Of course, profits of both these organizations are \$15 each, and they are the same amount as profits of the whole company. In this matrix income statement, profits of the whole company, not division profits, are calculated.

At first glance, ME uses "dual pricing," but this is the profit management system that ensures targeted profits for ME. Regularly, revenues and costs incurred by the divisions are contained in the division income statement. In the matrix income statement of ME, both managers of Works and Divisions understand how much profit they should make to make and sell products.

5. Discussions

A decentralized organization is often set as a profit center or an investment center. It independently operates and is expected to maximize profits. As mentioned before, it is generally said that divisions do not have a close relationship in many cases under the division system. In contrast, manufacturing and selling functions or vertically integrated divisions must work together to make profits, even though they are differentiated in an organization.

The more important thing is that this transfer pricing problem often happens in the division system. That is, products are transferred between a manufacturing department and a sales department in one division. Of course, division managers have a responsibility to make profits. They lead manufacturing department managers to make highly functional products with high quality at low costs, and they lead sales department managers to sell products on a budget.

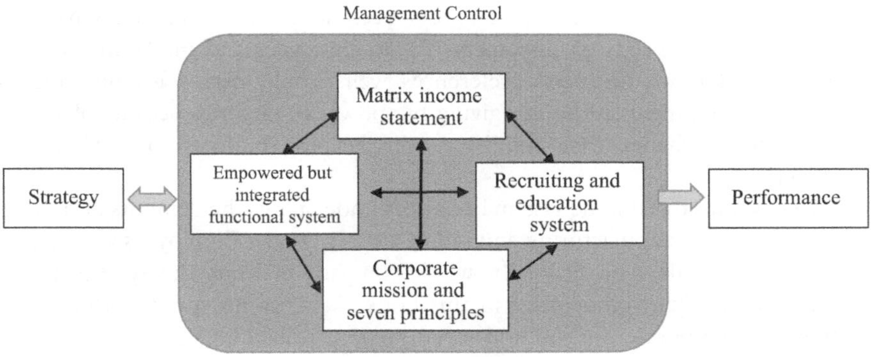

Figure 9.2 Strategic implementing system in ME

How does a division make profits? Although there are so many functions including R&D, logistics, and HR in a company, manufacturing and selling functions are critical. Just making products does not generate profits. Profits are not generated until the products are sold. In fact, a company obtains profits through making and selling products. A company cannot separate manufacturing and selling functions, and both managers of manufacturing and sales consider what to do and how to do it in order to maximize profits of the whole company.

The matrix income statement of ME is the tool for collaboration between manufacturing and selling functions. A manufacturing department and a selling department share the profitability of a product. Of course, a manufacturing manager does not have any authority to control costs in a selling department, and a sales manager does not have any authority to control costs in a manufacturing department. However, both divisions share all accounting information of their products to make profits. If the profits in the matrix income statement do not seem to reach the targeted profits, both departments start to consider what they should do. First, a manufacturing department tries to cut manufacturing costs and its management costs, and a selling department also tries to cut its costs as well as to sell more products. Second, they deliberate what features they need to add to their products if they are not competitive with rival products. This is an important example of "the horizontal interaction" that I explained in Chapter 2. Organizations in ME are empowered to operate by themselves but are highly integrated to accomplish their goal.

It is not meaningful for functional departments to measure profits. They have an important role to make profits, but they cannot do it by themselves. Hitachi used to set factories as profit centers. At that time factories had strong power over R&D, manufacturing, and even pricing. However, that worked more poorly little by little because this system was effective only under stable situations. During the economic boom in Japan from the 1960s to the middle of the

1980s, companies concentrated on keeping production to fulfill demands within cost budgets. As customers' preferences become diverse, companies have to meet the diverse needs of customers. To do this, sales and marketing departments that know customers' preferences well should play a leading role in product development. Although giving big power to factories became obsolete, they failed to change their mind-set from keeping budgets to seeking new products.

ME develops this unique system because it understands the demerits of transfer pricing between manufacturing and selling departments.[7] Employees also understand how to make a profit for the whole company by using this system. However, differing from other cases in this book, ME has no specific educational system of a corporate mission and seven guiding principles.

Notes

1 Direct material costs are variable costs.
2 Direct labor costs are fixed costs. Direct labor costs per hour of product X are calculated as total labor costs in division A, 1,000,000 yen, divided by total labor hours, 1,000 hours. Direct labor costs per hour of product Y are calculated as total labor costs in division B, 1,000,000 yen, divided by total labor hours, 1,000 hours.
3 Variable overhead costs per hour in division A are 400 yen and those in division B are 1,000 yen.
4 In Japanese, they are called "Seisaku-jo."
5 In Japanese, they are called "Jigyo-bu." In English, "a division" has all functions of operation and management, but a division of ME is just a selling department.
6 Works sometimes sell their products directly to customers.
7 NEC Corporation also found this problem, and it stopped transferring profits.

References

Anthony, R.N., J. Dearden, and N.M. Bedford (1989) *Management Control Systems*, 6th edition, Homewood, IL: R.D. Irwin.

Benk, R.N. Jr. and J.D. Edwards (1980) *Transfer Pricing: Techniques and Uses*, New York, NY: American Accounting Association.

Dejong, D., R. Forsythe, J.D. Kim, and W.C. Uecker (1989) A laboratory investigation of alternative transfer pricing mechanisms, *Accounting, Organizations and Society*, 14(1/2), 41–64.

Eccles, R.G. (1985) *The Transfer Pricing Problem: A Theory for Practice*, New York, NY: Lexington Book.

Horngren, T.H., S.M. Datar, and M. Rajan (2012) *Cost Accounting: A Managerial Emphasis*, 14th edition, Upper Saddle River, NJ: Prentice Hall.

Kaplan, R.S. (1988) *Advanced Management Accounting*, 2nd edition, Englewood Cliffs, NJ: Prentice-Hall.

Ronen, J. and K.R. Balachandran (1988) An approach to transfer pricing under uncertainty, *Journal of Accounting Research*, 26(2), 300–314.

Ronen, J. and K.R. Mckinney, III (1970) Transfer pricing for divisional autonomy, *Journal of Accounting Research*, 8(1), 99–112.

10 Beyond budgeting or new budgeting? The case of Disco

Key learning points

- What is beyond budgeting?
- Understand three main tools of beyond budgeting: relative goals, holistic approach to rewards, and rolling forecast.
- Learn why Disco abolishes the budgeting system and how to manage its operations without the budgeting system.

1. Introduction

This chapter deals with a budgeting system. Almost all organizations have been using budgeting since it was developed. Although it is a very useful management control tool, not only scholars but also practitioners criticize it strongly for several reasons. This has led a team to develop new management thought called *beyond budgeting* to overcome the dysfunction of budgeting. Jeremy Hope and Robin Fraser established the beyond budgeting round table (BBRT) in 1997, after they studied the alternatives to budgeting systems at the Consortium of Advanced Management, International (CAM-I).

They reached a decision to abolish budgeting systems after researching some companies that improved their management systems (Hope and Fraser, 2003a,b). To take some examples, companies that abolished budgeting systems are Rhodia, Borealis, and Svenska Handelsbanken. Particularly Handelsbanken, a Swedish commercial bank, has been managing its operations without budgeting for more than 40 years. Hope and Fraser visited these companies to theorize about a new management system that does not use budgeting systems. After that, some researchers and practitioners took over the study and the propagation of the idea of beyond budgeting from them.

I have been studying the beyond budgeting model (BBM) since 2003 and have found that some Japanese companies innovated on their budgeting systems. Some companies do not use budgeting systems at all, and others use an alternative to budgeting systems or introduced some idea of BBM.

This chapter provides an overview of the beyond budgeting model and introduces to readers a Japanese company, Disco, that abolished budgeting systems.

2. Theory of beyond budgeting

Research on beyond budgeting

The first paper and book on the beyond budgeting model (BBM) were published in 2003 (Hope and Fraser, 2003a,b). They propose that companies must build an adaptive and decentralized organization to overcome trouble with budgeting systems and implement their strategies successfully. From the point of view of practitioners, Neely et al. (2001) list 12 problems with budgeting systems. Hansen et al. (2003, pp. 96–97) categorize these problems into three elements. The first element is related to turbulent circumstances around companies. Managers forecast circumstances of the following year and make a budget. However, in the turbulent era, their plans based on the forecast often become obsolete when the next fiscal year starts because the forecast was made three to four months before the next fiscal year. Second, budgeting systems impose a command-and-control structure. Under rapidly changing circumstances, managers and employees need to think about how to contribute to making a profit by themselves. Budgeting systems make them focus on only keeping budgets, not implementing strategies. Third, the second problems make it impossible for companies to build adaptive and decentralized organizations that are highly empowered.

In unpredictable, non-contiguously changing environments, companies must step forward to make a flexible and quick decision. Hope and Fraser sought companies in Europe that introduced an innovation in budgeting systems, and finally found that some companies such as Svenska Handelsbanken[1] abolished them to improve their management control.

Hope and Fraser summarize 12 principles to introduce BBM: six adaptive processes and six radical decentralization principles. Later, Bogsnes[2] marshals and rebuilds them, as shown in Table 10.1.[3]

Table 10.1 Beyond budgeting concept

Leadership principles		
1	Customers	Focus everyone on improving customer outcomes, not on hierarchical relationships.
2	Organization	Organize as a network of lean, accountable teams, not around centralized functions.
3	Responsibility	Enable everyone to act and think like a leader, not merely follow the plan.
4	Autonomy	Give teams the freedom and capability to act; do not micromanage them.
5	Values	Govern through a few clear values, goals, and boundaries, not detailed rules and budgets.
6	Transparency	Promote open information for self-management; do not restrict it hierarchically.

Process principles		
7	Goals	Set relative goals for continuous improvement; do not negotiate fixed performance contracts.
8	Rewards	Reward shared success based on relative performance, not a top-down annual event.
9	Planning	Make planning a continuous and inclusive process, not based on variances against the plan.
10	Controls	Base controls on relative indicators and trends, not on variances against the plan.
11	Resources	Make resources available as needed, not through annual budget allocations.
12	Coordination	Coordinate interactions dynamically, not through annual planning cycles.

(Bogsnes, 2009, p. 55)

Process principles

If you would like to have some tools to overcome problems with budgeting systems, you should read and understand process principles. They include some specific tools to manage operations in companies. I select three tools – relative goals or targets, a holistic approach to rewards, and rolling forecasts – and explain them in the following sections.

Relative goals or targets

Goals must be set as relative goals. Generally, managers set goals or targets by the beginning of the new financial year based on their forecast of the coming year. Because managers' ability to meet their goals or not is directly tied to their bonus or other rewards in the United States, they often set goals that are easy to attain. This brings organizations notorious "budget gaming" and time-consuming negotiations. To avoid this problem, companies should use relative goals or targets. For example, a company may set an ROI or ROE target and compare it with the target of competitors. The target is the specific rank in the "league table." Take the case in which a company's ROE has a moderate rating in the industry. The CEO of the company hopes to raise its rank to the top three of this industry in three years. Even in this case, this CEO needs to set the specific target for profits (and net capital) initially, like budgeting systems. Even if the company's target is achieved, this company would lose when the top three competitors achieved a higher ROE. To outperform competitors, it is not enough for this company to achieve the initial target. The CEO always must attempt to beat competitors.

Companies use such "relative targets" in organizations. In Handelsbanken, "regions compete with each other on ROE and on the cost-to-income ratio" (Hope and Fraser, 2003b, p. 61) at the regional bank level, and the central office makes the league table of these measures. Region managers must compete with others in performance. However, their performance is disclosed after a fiscal year or a quarter finishes. Managers try to do their best at all times, because even though they accomplish the initial target, other managers may outperform them. In this case, there is no budgeting game in which managers try to set lower targets than what they actually expect. The ranking is not related to rewards. This will be explained in the next section.

Holistic approach to rewards

It is generally said that companies use the pay-per-performance system in many countries. This system leads managers and employees to dysfunctional activities because they intend to set easy targets (lower targets) for themselves. In this context, rewards mean a bonus.

Of course, this type of reward is appropriate in investment banks and securities firms because the performance of traders affects the whole company's financial results. However, management and operations are very complicated today. Companies make many teams, and one team cooperates with other teams to make a good performance for their company. In this situation, it is considered unsuitable to give rewards only for the performance of an individual person. Rewards are paid based on the performance of a team, group, or division, and the biggest category is "the performance of the whole company." Hope and Fraser show that Handelsbanken has a group-wide profit-sharing scheme in which the amount of bonus is decided by the total profit of this bank, although it makes the league table of some KPIs at a branch level and a region level (Hope and Fraser, 2003b, p. 76). It means the performance of managers at each level does not affect their bonuses. Actually, most Japanese companies adopt this scheme. The amount of bonuses is generally calculated as the base salary times several months that are decided by the profits of the previous year. This may differ depending on an employee, manager, and division, but the difference is very small. They often use the multilevel performance as a basis for each manager. Managers' bonuses are decided based on "their personal performance appraisal, the performance of their business unit, and the performance of the firm as a whole" (Hope and Fraser, 2003b, p. 76).

The merit of this system is to lead all employees to engage in good performance for their company. The demerit is that it enables many free riders who think that they can gain rewards even if they do not work hard. There may be another bigger problem. This system is not acceptable to some nations because they think they should receive a bonus based on their performance. If they achieve good performance, of course they must be given more rewards.

To overcome the first demerit, the league table is effective even though it is not related to a bonus. When the league table is open and the performance of managers is in the lower half every month, who can pass their time in idleness? It is uncontradictable that there are some persons who do not dedicate themselves to their work very much and do not mind the ranking, although they are a minority group.

As for division managers who earn better profits, they contribute to company profits by increasing their profits. As for managers who suffer deficits, they contribute to company profits by decreasing their deficits.

This solution is effective only with regard bonuses. Concerning a promotion and a rise in salary, we need another system to evaluate managers' performance from various perspectives, such as financial performance, making applicable action plans to implement strategy, fulfilling those action plans efficiently, and the result of peer review.

The second demerit is difficult to solve. This often occurs in the situation that Japanese companies expand their operations overseas and establish subsidiaries in other countries. A possible solution is to have a different evaluation system, but this does not fundamentally solve the problem. The most effective and only one solution is that top management has managers and employees develop the consciousness that they should maximize company-wide profits and share them. Toyota and Kyocera succeed in doing that outside Japan. However, many other companies seem to fail to do so.

Rolling forecast

A rolling forecast is related to planning, controls, and resources of process principles (Table 10.1). The feedback system is not sufficient to attain good performance because it starts when something is done and results are compared with targets. Sometimes it is too late. Under turbulent conditions, companies must take advantage of the feedforward system. Concretely speaking, rolling forecasts are necessary to attain relative targets in the feedforward system.

Rolling forecasts are a forecasting system in which companies "continuously look five or six quarters ahead" (Bogsnes, 2009, p. 43) or 12 months ahead, as shown in Figure 10.1. If the forecast of profits, especially one at the end of the fiscal year, does not seem to reach the target, it is a good trigger for companies to take new action to recover their performance. Rolling forecasts also need to use a relative target. As explained previously, relative targets are set as the specific ranking of a KPI or KPIs in an industry or in a company. To attain relative targets, managers need to know their future status as well as their current ranking. As shown in Chapter 4, Japanese companies use the rolling forecast

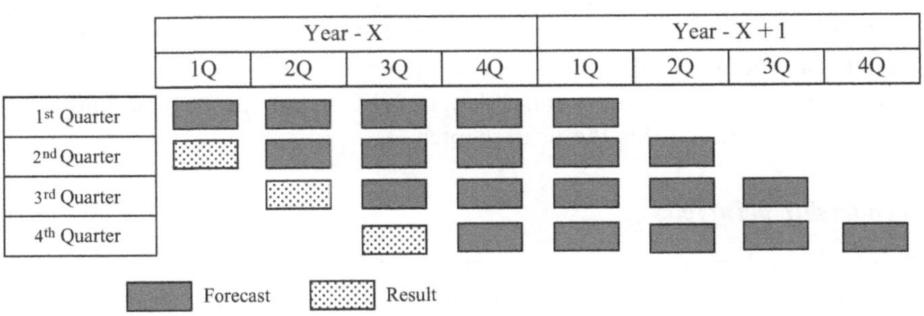

Figure 10.1 Rolling forecast

	1Q	2Q	3Q	4Q	1Q	2Q
May	✓					
June	✓	✓	*			
July		✓				
August		✓				
September		✓	✓	✓		
October			✓	✓		
November			✓	✓		
December			✓	✓	*	
January				✓	*	
February				✓	*	
March				✓	*	

Figure 10.2 Forecast system in NEC
(Sekizawa, 2013)

system, but many of their systems are rolling forecasts of the end of the fiscal year, not of the next four or five quarters.

NEC Corporation learned the beyond budgeting model and introduced the forecast system as shown in Figure 10.2.

The fiscal year of NEC is from April to March. NEC forecasts seven KPIs, the amount of orders received, sales, operating income, income before taxes, cash flow, cash conversion cycle, and expenses. It forecasts these KPIs of the end of the first quarter (June) in May. If there are gaps between these forecasts and targets, managers of NEC start to consider action plans to fill these gaps and to attain the targets. In June, the last month of the first quarter, NEC forecasts seven KPIs of the next quarter as well as those of the first quarter. In addition, it forecasts the sales of the third quarter. The asterisk in Figure 10.2 means that NEC forecasts the sales. As seen in Figure 10.2, the forecast system of NEC is a type of rolling forecast even though it is imperfect, and it is much better than the system that forecasts only the end of the fiscal year. The forecast system of Kyocera is more advanced than NEC's and the beyond budgeting model. I will explain this the next chapter.

Leadership principles

Leadership principles are more subjective and implicit than process principles. Mainly they focus on attitudes and motivations of managers and employees, and corporate culture. Management control systems include these points, but it is a bit difficult to explain them scientifically because they are closely connected to human psychology. Also, it is not true that companies only need to introduce these six processes. Whether organizations succeed in attaining good performance by using some of the six processes depends on the motivation of managers and employees to implement those processes successfully. In other words, if managers' and employees' ways of thinking are backward-looking, processes and tools will have no effect on their performance.

Value

It is very important that companies have a good mission to resonate with managers and employees in order to make them positive and forward-looking. A good mission inspires people and leads them to work hard in the right way. It is not sufficient that companies proclaim their mission with beautiful words. An inspiring mission of companies is often based on the belief and the motto of the distinguished founders or top management of these companies. Based on the founders' belief and motto, the mission is then explained to all people in the company.

To have a good mission is not sufficient. A good mission facilitates employees doing their work successfully. It leads to appropriate behavior. However, companies must also have the system that prevents managers and employees from doing wrong things, as well as the system that assists their good behavior. Companies have a code of conduct that makes to-do and not-to-do lists. A not-to-do list includes rules and manners to avoid sub-optimized behavior.

Transparency and trust

Once all managers and employees fully embrace a good mission, companies should trust them and disclose all information to assist them in self-governing activities. Even though people are capable and skilled, and would like to align with a company's goals, they cannot do anything without information about the business. Particularly, when companies use relative goals and a holistic approach to bonuses, people need to know exact information about companies' forecasted KPIs and rankings on the league table. Many companies do not disclose important information about their business because they do not trust managers and employees. However, companies must not limit their actions by not informing. Many senior executives claim that not all employees are trustworthy and managers in each organizational hierarchy should have only information within their authority. It is true that some managers may deceive their bosses to give themselves the advantage, although they are a minority.

I do not mean that companies can neglect those managers. Generally, lazy employees do not obtain good evaluations, nor are they promoted not only in Japanese society but in American and European society. In addition, these employees are punished socially in the Japanese social control system. Most of the employees are dedicated to their job and capable of working. First of all, companies should motivate these good employees by empowering and informing.

3. The company outline

The history of Disco[4]

Disco was founded in 1937 by Mitsuo Sekiya as a small manufacturer of abrasive tools. In the beginning, it developed an abrasive wheel just 1.2 millimeters thick in 1950 and gradually expanded its business into abrasives used for tube glass, silicon, and other materials in the 1960s. In the 1970s, Disco reached a threshold. There was no slicing machine that fully utilized the performance of its abrasives, and machine manufacturers always held Disco responsible for troubles. Thus, Disco made a decision to develop and produce slicing machines by itself. It produced an automatic scriber/dicing saw in 1975 and the first fully automatic dicing saw in the world in 1978. Since then, it has improved its products by downsizing, cutting costs, and introducing new technologies.

Current major products and services of Disco are as follows (http://www.disco.co.jp/eg/ corporate/outline/index.html):

1. Manufacture and sale of precision cutting, grinding, and polishing machines
2. Maintenance of precision cutting, grinding, and polishing machines
3. Training in the operation and maintenance of precision cutting, grinding, and polishing machines
4. Disassembly and recycling of precision cutting, grinding, and polishing machines
5. Lease of precision machines and sale and purchase of used machines
6. Manufacture and sale of precision diamond abrasive tools
7. For-fee processing

Financial performance

Financial performance of the fiscal year 2014 and 2015 is shown in Table 10.2. The remarkable characteristic of the financial performance of Disco is high

Table 10.2 Financial performance of Disco

Net sales		*Operating income*		*Net income after tax*	
Millions of yen		*Millions of yen*		*Millions of yen*	
2015	*2014*	*2015*	*2014*	*2015*	*2014*
127,850	125,920	30,338	26,760	23,092	20,087

Adapted from http://www.disco.co.jp/eg/ir/library/pd23.7f/fr/fr20160511.pdf

profitability. Its ROS (operating income divided by net sales) in 2015 is 23.7 percent, and is much higher than that of average Japanese manufacturers.

Corporate mission

The mission of Disco is "bringing science to comfortable living through advanced *Kiru, Kezuru* and *Migaku* technologies" (http://www.disco.co.jp/eg/corporate/values/index. html). This mission consists of English and Japanese, "Kiru, Kezuru, and Migaku." The meaning of Kiru is "cut," Kezuru is "grind," and Migaku is "polish." According to this website, the reason why Disco writes its mission in English and Japanese is that it hopes its technology will be global standards and the Japanese words "Kiru, Kezuru, and Migaku" will be understood all over the world.

Disco states its Disco Values to achieve its mission. Disco Values "represent the corporate philosophy that identifies the ideal from various perspectives, including the direction in which the company should progress, the basic approach of management, and the manner in which each and every employee works" (http://www.disco.co.jp/eg/corporate/ values/index.html). When companies are small, people from top management to front-line employees discuss the future of their companies and understand the situation of companies. As the scale of companies becomes larger, many employees cannot grasp companies' circumstances and do not understand their strategy. Thus "desiring to regain the shared values it had had when it was smaller, in 1995 Disco launched Future Project Alpha, aimed at top management" (http://www.disco.co.jp/eg/corporate/history/ period6.html). The Disco Values consist of over 200 items, and Disco is committed to have all employees understand Disco Values fully.

Disco attributes an increase in its corporate value to the improvement of the feasibility of its mission and the enhancement of an exchange value, as shown in Figure 10.3. Take a look at the right side of Figure 10.3. To increase a

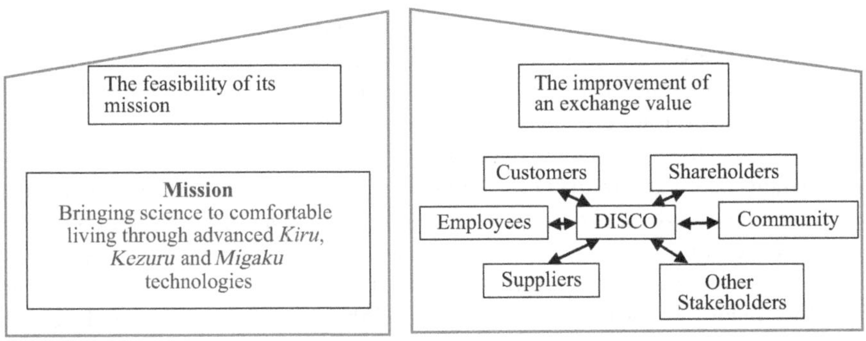

Figure 10.3 Increasing corporate value
(Kobayashi, 2016, p. 25)

corporate value, Disco makes efforts to enhance an "exchange value" with all stakeholders (even though priority is given to customers).

To spread these ideas throughout the company, Disco has many chances to have employees contact with the Disco Values. For example, the Disco Values are incorporated in its annual management policy and are taught in seminars for all employees.

4. The management system in Disco

Disco abolished the budgeting system in 2013. Customers of Disco are mainly chip manufacturers and electronic components manufacturers. Because these manufacturers can be subject to business fluctuations, their orders change dramatically. The forecasts used in budgeting became obsolete immediately after the budget was made. As a consequence, no one took notice of the budget nor controlled it. The reason why Disco kept making the budget lies in the rule of "Disclosure of Earnings Forecast" at the Tokyo Stock Exchange. This rule required that listed companies disclose the forecast of sales, operating income, and other data in the following fiscal year.[5] Disco disclosed its forecast, but the result substantially differed from it. Therefore, Disco had to revise its forecast every quarter. Business environments surrounding Disco made it more difficult to forecast future performance and to control the implementation of a fixed target. Disco introduced "Will Accounting" to work through this problem, to meet quick and enormous demand fluctuations, and to make a flexible organization. Will Accounting is a concept that "every organization autonomously pursues the best activity for the company."[6]

Finally, Disco decided to stop making a budget. The following is a story of "beyond budgeting" in Disco.

Relative target

What is a target in Disco if it does not make a budget? It does not have any fixed targets. In fact, there is no sales target nor cost target set at the beginning of the year. The target is return on sales[7] of a four-year moving average. The target of ROS is 20 percent. Disco adopted the amoeba system (see Chapter 11) but felt it inconvenient to keep using this system and introduced a new system. The notable purpose of this new system is to encourage all employees to do their best all the time even in turbulent circumstances.

For a sales division, market share is an important KPI. There are fewer customers and manufactures in Disco's business area than other business areas such as automobile and electronic industries. Thus the sales force of Disco always competes with the same rivals at a sale destination. The sales force tries to take orders by responding to customer needs. It is interesting that it reports the win-loss record of orders. No members of the sales force hope to lose and commit themselves to taking best actions for customers and for Disco itself.

Back-office employees voluntarily intend to control their costs in a positive way. Disco discloses a year-end forecasted ROS to all employees every quarter.

If the forecast of ROS is unfavorable, back-office employees consider cutting their costs. Employees do not just postpone paying nonurgent expenses but also consider changing their work that causes these expenses. They must research why they incur costs and remove the cause of them.

Holistic approach to rewards

Why do employees in Disco intend to cut costs when the forecast of ROS is not good? There are two reasons. One is a bonus system. The bonus system in Disco uses the holistic approach rather than the pay-per-performance approach. The amount of the bonus is preliminarily decided – for example, employees receive a bonus equivalent to a given number of months' salary when targeted ROS is accomplished. Each employee's performance is reflected in his or her bonus, but the amount of this portion is small. Of course, because employees hope to get more bonus, they are anxious to attain the targeted ROS by doing everything they can do to cut costs. However, this approach needs a mechanism that keeps employees from partaking opportunistic activities and free riding. Disco Values and some systems based on it play an important role in avoiding these inadequate activities.

Performance Innovation Management

Performance Innovation Management (PIM) is the second reason for cutting costs. Disco started PIM in 2004. The purpose of this system is to have employees consider what the best activity is and change their activity for the company. Disco uses PIM to improve operations every day. Under PIM, employees focus not only on result indicators but on performance drivers. Disco calls these performance drivers realizing indicators (Kizuki indicators). By using realizing indicators, Disco asks all employees to lead the company into the best condition. Thus, Disco does not ask employees just to temporarily save money and postpone spending money, but to cut costs structurally and permanently. All employees try to find realizing indicators to realize optimum conditions and to improve their activities. Finally, these ways of thinking lead employees to consider structural and permanent cost-cutting.

In the stuff department (e.g., accounting and corporate planning), employees are required to reduce working hours to improve their productivity. However, reducing employee working hours from 10 to 9 does not reduce costs until a company reduces its workforce. Employees can do new work to contribute to the whole company's profits by using saved hours. This means the PIM is aimed at making new profits.

Painful Charge / Will Reward

In addition to these systems, Disco has a unique system to assist employees in considering optimum activities. It's the Painful Charge / Will Reward system.

When a subunit (or an employee) takes any actions that have a negative impact on corporate profits, a fine (Painful Charge) is imposed on this subunit (or this employee). In contrast, when a subunit (or an employee) takes any actions that have a positive impact on corporate profits, a Will Reward is given. Painful Charges and Will Rewards are paid and received virtual money, but they are reflected in the financial performance of subunits.[8] The purpose of a Painful Charge is to have a subunit that has problems and inefficiency recognize the trend and be encouraged to improve. For example, let us assume that a sales department accepts some changes to the specification. A designing department and a trial manufacturing department must make a change in their work, and it causes additional costs. And if a sales department accepts a change in the terms of delivery as told by a customer, production scheduling will become confused. Sales departments must avoid these problems by communication with and observation of customers. When these troubles occur, a sales department must pay a Painful Charge to a manufacturing department, and this amount is reflected in the income statement of both departments.

A way of setting the amount of a Painful Charge is interesting. It is set by discussion between interested departments (a sales department and a manufacturing department in this case) without gaming. The reason why they do the right thing is that Disco Values tell all employees what to do and what not to do. Disco Values play a critical role.

5. Discussion

I mentioned in Chapter 4 that beyond budgeting is not effective in Japanese companies and the KPI forecast management model is needed. For not only companies in Japan but also those in the United States and European countries, abolishing the budgeting system causes trouble over planning and control. Managers and employees do not know how to set their targets and cannot measure their performance without budgets. Therefore, companies adopting beyond budgeting models use some control systems as a substitute for the budgeting system. In addition to these control systems, it is necessary to develop a system to motivate people to do the right thing. Top management should tell all people in their company to do the right thing and compete with rivals in the right manner, as well as trust managers and employees, and empower them to make some decisions. Top management must set an inspiring corporate philosophy or mission to guide people to think and do the right thing. As mentioned previously, there are so many barriers to the implementation of a beyond budgeting model. Only companies famous for beyond budgeting, such as Handelsbanken and Statoil, overcome those barriers. However, it is difficult for most companies to do that. Thus I propose the KPI forecast management model. It is useful for companies to obtain better control of their budgeting system and, in fact, most Japanese companies have some aspects of the KPI forecast management model as seen in Chapter 4. This is a practical solution to the problems with budgeting.

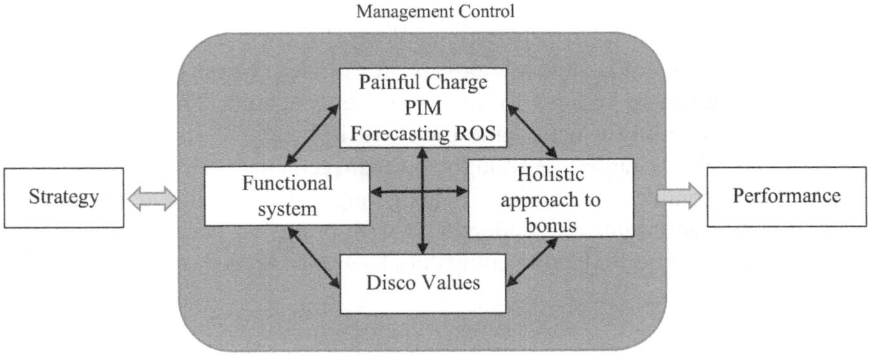

Figure 10.4 Strategic implementing system in Disco

However, I do not intend to prevent companies from stopping to use the budgeting system. If a company does not need to make a budget, it is no problem that this company stops using a budget. Disco is certainly applicable to this case. Disco makes a budget to disclose forecast information, but nobody controls it because it is useless in turbulent business environments. The challenge of Disco is a model case of the beyond budgeting model. As far as I know, Disco is the only company that utilizes the concept of the beyond budgeting model in Japan.

The basic policy in Disco is that "all employees try their best" for the company. They have the authority to consider what the best thing is for the company. Why do they take this attitude? Because they know that trying everything encourages the development of their skills as well as contributes to company profits. Employees also know that when they contribute toward making profits, the company rewards them. The holistic system for bonuses is suitable for this situation.

Disco has specific management accounting tools such as the Painful Charge / Will Reward system and PIM. The Painful Charge / Will Reward system may seem to be the result of control systems from the perspective of Merchant and Van der Stede. Employees are rewarded when they contribute to other divisions and departments. This leads to company profits. In contrast, they must pay the penalty when they bring trouble to other employees. The purpose of this system is to have employees consider what activities bring benefits to the company and what activities destroy its value. PIM also plays an important role in awaking employees to the fact that activities are critical to the long-term optimization of the company.

Disco Values are the base of all activities in Disco. It is easy for many companies to introduce these systems, like the many tools discussed in BBM. However, they are not effective until people's mind-set in a company changes from individualism or opportunism to healthy thought, by which they always consider optimization. Employees are not moved just by management control tools; companies need to generate an excellent philosophy or mission, and top management must make it penetrate employees' consciousness.

I mentioned that it is almost impossible for modern companies to stop using the budgeting system because it brings chaos to companies. Therefore, Japanese companies keep using it with some tools in BBM, such as the rolling forecast system and relative targets. Although top management in Disco did not learn BBM, Disco completely abolished its budgeting system because it became useless. If a company thinks the budgeting system brings no benefit, abolishing it, as Disco and beyond budgeting companies have experienced, will be a workable alternative.

Notes

1 Handelsbanken stopped using its budgeting system in the 1970s. It focuses on customers, gives greater authority to branches and regions, makes management data transparent, and has a holistic approach to bonuses (Bogsnes, 2009).
2 He is the BBRT chairman and is a project manager of Statoil's beyond budgeting project.
3 BBRT improves additionally 12 principles in 2011 (http://beyondbudgeting.org/ beyond-budgeting/bb-principles.html). Leadership principles include values, governance, transparency, teams, trust, and accountability, and process principles include goals, rewards, planning, coordination, resources, and controls.
4 I use the following websites as references: http://www.disco.co.jp/eg/corporate/history/period1.html, http://www.disco.co.jp/jp/corporate/history/period2.html, http://www.disco.co.jp/eg/corporate/history/period3.html, http://www.disco.co.jp/jp/corporate/history/period4.html, http://www.disco.co.jp/jp/corporate/history/period5.html
5 This rule is relaxed now. Companies do not necessarily have to disclose performance forecasts due to the difficulty of forecasting performance in rapidly changing environments.
6 The case of Disco is based on an interview with Kazuo Kobayashi of Disco in 2012 (Shimizu, 2013).
7 Disco uses current profit (Net Sales – COGS – SGA + Non-Operating Income – Non-Operating Expense) as return in this equation. This is called Keijo-Rieki and is used broadly in Japan.
8 This system is extended to each employee.

References

Bogsnes, B. (2009) *Implementing Beyond Budgeting: Unlocking the Performance Potential*, Hoboken, NJ: John Wiley & Sons.

Hansen, S.C., D. Otley, and W. Van der Stede (2003) Practice development in budgeting: An overview and research perspective, *Journal of Management Accounting Research*, 15, 95–116.

Hope, J. and R. Fraser (2003a) Who needs budgets? *Harvard Business Review*, 81(2), 115–118.

Hope, J. and R. Fraser (2003b) *Beyond Budgeting: How Manager Can Break Free from the Annual Performance Trap*, Boston, MA: Harvard Business School Press.

Neely, A., M.R. Sutcliff, and H.R. Heyns (2001) *Driving Value through Strategic Planning and Budgeting*, New York, NY: Accenture.

Kobayashi, Y. (2016) *The Improvement of Organizational Behavior by Will Accounting*, The Handout of the Strategic Accounting Meeting at Business Research Institute. Written in Japanese.

Sekizawa, H. (2013), *The Consolidated Management in NEC*, Lecture material of 77th Cost Accounting Course at Sangyo-Keiri Kyokai. Written in Japanese.

Shimizu, T. (2013) The theory and practice of KPI forecast management, *Waseda Business Review* (Waseda University), 434, 511–540. Written in Japanese.

11 Microprofit centers

Amoeba system in Kyocera

Key learning points

- Microprofit centers are independent and empowered organizations.
- Kyocera uses the amoeba system as microprofit centers.
- Learn how Kyocera manages microprofit centers by using a self-supporting system, hourly efficiency, and a forecasting system.

1. Introduction

As shown in Chapter 10, the beyond budgeting model (BBM) was introduced by Hope and Fraser in 2003 (Hope and Fraser, 2003a,b). It is a type of change management model to help create an adaptive organization in which front-line employees are empowered to cope with recent turbulent management environments.

BBM is generally not accepted by Japanese companies, except for Disco. However, some companies have the same idea as BBM, using forecasts effectively to attain managers' targets, using relative targets and a holistic approach to bonuses and setting an influential code of conduct to support their good attitude.

Kyocera is a manufacturer of ceramics, semiconductors, and electronic devices. It does not use a budgeting system, although it has a strong financial control system. It is often said that strong financial control may cause suboptimal activities of mangers. Kyocera has some specific management tools and a philosophy to overcome this problem. I call this type of management model the KPI forecast management model. Its purpose is to achieve the goal of the BBM without stopping the budget itself or functions of budgeting.

In addition to this new model, the organization of Kyocera receives attention. In the theory, a profit center consists of all functions of a business. However, in Japan, functional departments, a sales department, and a manufacturing department are often set as a profit or an investment center. The dual transfer pricing system that Mitsubishi Electronic uses is devised to manage these functional departments in this situation. In Kyocera, small groups of a manufacturing line and a sales department are set as profit centers, and managers of these small groups are responsible for their group's profits, although the managers do not have all authority to make profits. Cooper (1995) calls these organizations "microprofit centers." In this chapter, I will introduce the features of microprofit centers and the Kyocera management model. I will also discuss ways in which the Kyocera management model has some similarities to the beyond budgeting model.

2. Theory of microprofit centers

The first author who introduced Microprofit Centers was Cooper (1995). He investigated some Japanese companies and found the distinctive feature of profit management – microprofit centers. A microprofit center means that companies divide a division or a department into small groups and make them into profit centers. Processes in the factory, groups in a sales force, and support departments may be set as microprofit centers. Cooper says that the advantages "derive from the creation of increased responsibility and the awareness this brings to group members of the effect of their actions on the profitability of the firm" (Cooper, 1995, p. 279). Leaders of microprofit centers do not simply reduce costs. They know that they can contribute toward making profits, and this consciousness motivates them to make profits.

Cooper classifies a microprofit center into two types: a pseudomicroprofit center and a real microprofit center. The former is an organization whose leaders do not have all kinds of decision-making authority, with prices, product mix, and volume of manufacture (Cooper and Kaplan, 1998). In contrast, the latter is a "real" profit center that is segmentalized into small groups. The reason why leaders of these groups are committed to increasing their profits with limited decision-making authority is that "these systems provide real psychological benefits by focusing the teams on the positive action of increasing profits as opposed to the negative action of decreasing or avoiding costs" (Cooper and Kaplan, 1998, p. 65). Beyond controversy, empowerment is required to make microprofit centers function effectively.

Inspired by Cooper (1995) and Cooper and Kaplan (1998), many researchers conduct studies of microprofit centers in Japan. The features found by these studies are as follows: all small organizations have their income statement and get feedback from the information on it; these income statements are open in a company and all small organizations compete with each other; leaders of small groups are empowered to improve their financial performance; and in many cases, financial performance of small groups is not directly linked with the leaders' bonus, but a company has a system to commend leaders and members of a group for good performance instead.

These features are similar to those of the BBM we learned in Chapter 10. Next I will tell you how Kyocera operates amoeba organizations as microprofit centers, and compare them with the BBM.

3. The company outline

The history of Kyocera

Kyocera Corporation was founded by Kazuo Inamori in 1959 as a fine ceramics manufacturer. It was a very small factory at the beginning. Inamori was committed to his business and led the company to success. It opened a resident office in California in 1968, and was listed in Japan in 1971 and in New York in 1980. Inamori is one of the top management leaders in Japan. His belief is based on trust in employees and it is presented in the Kyocera management rationale: "to provide opportunities for the material and intellectual growth of all our employees, and through our joint efforts, contribute to the advancement of society and humankind" (http://global.kyocera.com/ company/philosophy/ index.html). Like other senior managers of large companies in Japan, he seems to be influenced by Konosuke Matsushita, the founder of Panasonic.

Major products of Kyocera are as follows (http://global.kyocera.com/ company/summary/ company_profile.html):

1 Fine ceramics: Fine ceramic components and automotive components
2 Semiconductor components: Ceramic packages and substrates, organic packages and printed wiring boards, and organic materials
3 Electronic devices: Electronic components, crystal devices, connectors, displays, printing devices, and power semiconductors
4 Telecommunications equipment: Smartphones, feature phones, tablets, M2M modules
5 Information equipment: Printers and multifunctional products, and document solutions
6 Other businesses

Financial performance

Financial performance for fiscal year 2014 and 2015 is shown in Table 11.1. The noteworthy feature of the financial performance of Kyocera is that it has not suffered a deficit since the start of the business. From FY 2014 to FY 2015,

Table 11.1 Financial performance of Kyocera

Net sales		*Operating income*		*Net income after tax*	
Millions of yen		*Millions of yen*		*Millions of yen*	
2015	*2014*	*2015*	*2014*	*2015*	*2014*
1,479,627	1,526,536	92,656	93,428	109,047	115,875

Adapted from http://global.kyocera.com/ir/financial/pdf/rt160427_e.pdf

sales and profits decreased. Kyocera increased sales of products of automobiles and smartphones, but it recorded impairment loss in some business areas. Overall, financial performance grew steadily because sales for four years (from FY 2012 to FY 2016) increased by 15.6 percent and net income after tax increased by 64.0 percent.

Kyocera philosophy

Kyocera has very strong centripetal force. Its core is the Kyocera philosophy. Its corporate motto is "Respect the Divine and Love People," and its management system is based on the bonds that form among human minds. Kyocera also has 12 management principles, as shown in Table 11.2.

These principles form the basis of all employee behavior and penetrate deeply into all employees in such a way that they begin to understand the content of principles by training for new recruits and follow the principles when making decisions every day. As mentioned later, the Kyocera management model (KMM) is based on trust, but this trust is not created without the Kyocera philosophy.

Table 11.2 The 12 management principles in Kyocera

1	Clearly state the purpose and mission of your business. Set high objectives that are noble, just, and fair.
2	Set specific goals. Once targets are set, share them with all employees.
3	Keep a passionate desire in your heart. Your desire must be strong and persistent to penetrate into your subconscious mind.
4	Strive harder than anyone else. Work steadily and diligently, one step at a time, never relenting in tedious tasks.
5	Maximize revenues and minimize expenses. Measure your inflow and control your outflow; don't chase profit, but let it follow your effort.
6	Pricing is management. Pricing is top management's responsibility: to find that one point where customers are happy and the company is most profitable.
7	Success is determined by willpower. Business management requires a persistent, "rock-piercing" will.
8	Possess a fighting spirit. Management requires a more combative mentality than any material art.
9	Face every challenge with courage. Be fair and never deceive others.
10	Always be creative in your work. Innovate and improve continuously. Today should be better than yesterday; tomorrow, better than today.
11	Be kind and sincere. Business is based on partnerships and must bring happiness to all parties.
12	Always be cheerful and positive; hold great dreams and hopes in the pureness of your heart.

http://global.kyocera.com/inamori/management/twelve.html

4. The management system in Kyocera

Kyocera has its own management model called the ***amoeba management system.*** Kyocera abolished budgets and uses a ***master plan*** (MP) instead, which consists of three-year, annual, and monthly plans. Like BBM, this model motivates people to achieve a goal by using a forecast. Manufacturing and sales divisions are divided into small groups called amoebas in which amoeba leaders are empowered to operate their amoebas and are responsible for their profits. They control themselves by ***hourly efficiency*** (HE) and their income statement for internal use. Kyocera makes a league table of HE to encourage competition among amoebas. Each amoeba leader tries to make profits and improve its HE, but amoeba profits are not linked with employees' bonuses. In addition to these management tools, Kyocera has a very strong corporate philosophy and codes of conduct. They are extremely similar to the 12 principles of beyond budgeting in Chapter 11, although Kyocera has a typical financial plan, MP. I will compare the Kyocera management model (KMM) with BBM and consider the similarities between the two models in the next section.

Organization, responsibility, and autonomy principles

This section shows noteworthy features of trust and accountability given to the organization of Kyocera. Kyocera is composed of functional organizations. Production organizations and sales organizations are divided into small, autonomic, and empowered organizations, which are called ***amoebas.*** Production and sales amoebas are made up of 5 to 10 people each.

Each amoeba has an income statement and works as a profit center. However, the goal of each amoeba is to maximize profits of the whole company, not an individual, and to contribute to big profits.

Figure 11.1 shows the mechanism of management by a sales amoeba and production amoebas. First, a sales amoeba (SA) accepts an order from a customer

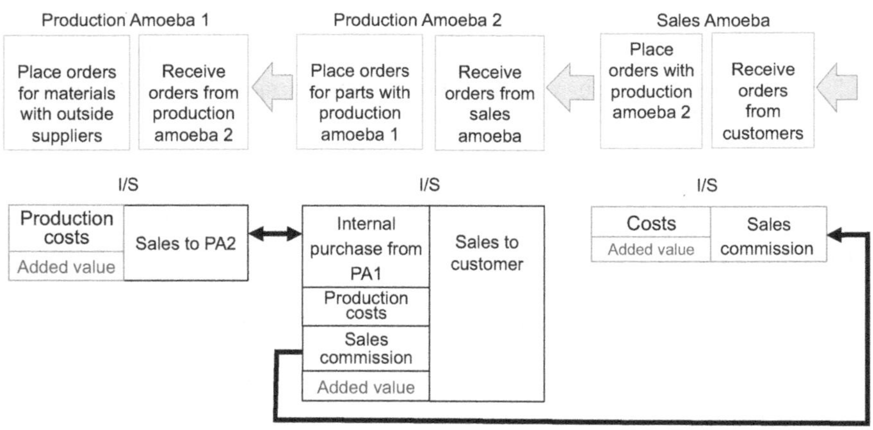

Figure 11.1 Sales amoeba and production amoeba

and passes it to a production amoeba 2 (PA2). The transfer price between SA and PA2 is the price that this SA receives from a customer. Next, the production amoeba 2 also places an order with PA1. PA1 and PA2 negotiate the transfer price so that both of them can earn profits.

After deciding the transfer price, every amoeba considers its own costs and working hours in order to maximize profits and HE. For SA, the selling price equals to the transfer price to PA2. PA2 pays the sales commission (e.g., 10 percent of total sales) to SA. SA tries to make profits and added value by controlling its costs. PA2 and PA1 also try to make profits by controlling their costs. I will explain this system and HE later.

The goal is to maximize profits of the whole company, not an amoeba. All the amoebas know the market price of their products. If sales amoebas put a low price on the products, they will win many orders, but it will be possibly unprofitable. In the contrary case, sales amoebas cannot win orders in the first place. Therefore, all the amoebas do not intend to set the price or transfer prices in their favor because it does not contribute toward able maximizing profits of the whole company. Kyocera has a pricing policy in which all the amoebas try to find the price that makes both customers (not only external customers but also internal customers, other amoebas) and Kyocera (or an amoeba) happy. In this way, Kyocera stops employees from making sub-optimized decisions.

All the amoebas take the optimum actions to maximize corporate profits like this. The amoebas are empowered to operate themselves. For example, the leaders of production amoebas even have the authority to invest in equipment when they judge that the investment can contribute to long-term profits.

The income statement and HE of each amoeba are disclosed at the review meeting. And at the meeting, an amoeba's leader has to explain what he/she did in order to maximize corporate profits and what the result was. HE is also disclosed to all employees with a league table.

Amoeba's income statement and HE

Table 11.3 is an example of the income statement made by production amoebas. HE is calculated as added value (7 in Table 11.3) divided by total working hours (8 in Table 11.3).

HE is set as a relative target. HE of all the amoebas is calculated and appears on the league table. An improvement in HE is not directly connected with bonuses of amoeba members and leaders, but they make efforts to improve HE and to raise their ranking on the league table like playing a game.

By the way, the income statement of the amoebas does not include labor costs. If labor costs are included in it, amoeba leaders may not select older employees as members. That is because Kyocera applies a seniority wage system in which the older the employee, the higher the salary they get. It is not good for Kyocera not to select older members because it focuses on "the bond of human minds."

Table 11.3 Income statement and hourly efficiency in production amoebas

	Items	*Amounts*
①=②+③	Gross production	6,500,000
②	Production outside	4,000,000
③	Total internal sales	2,500,000
④	Total internal purchases	2,200,000
⑤=①−④	Net production	4,300,000
⑥	Deduction (costs)	2,400,000
⑦=⑤−⑥	Added value	1,900,000
⑧	Total working hours	35,000 hours
⑨=⑦÷⑧	Hourly efficiency	54.28
⑩=⑤÷⑧	Production per hour	122.85

Adapted from http://global.kyocera.com/inamori/management/amoeba/system.html

Thus, Kyocera calculates only total (company-wide) labor costs and "labor costs per hour" (LCPH) of the whole company and gives this information to all the amoebas. An amoeba makes a comparison between the company-wide LCPH and its HE, and when its HE is larger than the company-wide LCPH, it means that this amoeba contributes to company-wide profits.

Master plan and forecasted income statement – Planning and control

Kyocera makes a three-year master plan (mp) as a rolling system. Based on the three-year MP, it makes an annual MP and then deploys it to a monthly MP.

The most remarkable feature of the Kyocera management system is the way of realizing the monthly MP. I will explain it with Table 11.4.

What action will amoeba leaders take if they find that the forecasted profits may not reach profits in MP? First they probably try to increase the sales volume. However, if customers (or other amoebas) do not place an order, the sales volume does not increase. Increasing the production volume without orders just causes an increase in bad inventories. Therefore, production amoeba leaders often visit their customers with sales persons, and take an order by researching customers' needs and making suggestions for them. Still, if the profit target is not achieved, the amoeba leaders work furiously to reduce costs even though the costs are included in MP, and aim to achieve the profit target.

This income statement is reported monthly at the performance review meeting. Amoeba leaders and senior managers are required to give an explanation in detail about the performance for the previous month and the plan for this month. They are always required to produce the best figure and their minds are also encouraged to do that by Kyocera philosophy. If an amoeba leader sets a low target and makes an income statement easy to realize, his or her intention will be exposed to other leaders and managers at the performance review meeting and he or she will be urged to modify the income statement. This is also connected with the transparency principle in BBM.

Forecasting system

As shown in Table 11.4, the income statement of each amoeba has an MP and a plan. Amoeba leaders have to forecast sales and costs for the next two months. As shown in Figure 11.2, this system is a three-month-rolling forecast. Amoeba leaders formulate a plan of the next month based on MP, forecasting the results of the next month. Although amoeba leaders are required to attain targets in MP, when the forecasted results fall below the target, they set a new plan (PLN in Figure 11.2). Amoeba leaders also forecast all items of Income Statement the following two months (FCT in Figure 11.2). For example, in April they formulate a new plan for May and make a forecast about all items of the income statement for June and July. Based on these new plans and forecasted items, amoeba leaders make efforts to accomplish targets in MP. However, there are a few exceptions. In July, an amoeba does not forecast the income statement in October because it has already started to forecast the income statement of the second half year. After predicting IS of the second half year, the amoeba sets a revised MP.

The integration of feedforward and feedback management

The Kyocera system consists of both feedforward and feedback management. First, each amoeba forecasts and makes a new plan to accomplish its MP. It is

Table 11.4 Forecasted income statement of production amoebas

	MP	*Plan*	*Difference*	*Actual*	*Action*
Gross production					
Total internal sales					
Net production					
Deduction (costs)					
...					
...					
...					
Added value					
Total working hours					
Hourly efficiency					

Adapted from Miya, H., *The Theory of AMOEBA Management*, Toyokeizai-Shinpousha (2003, p. 93)

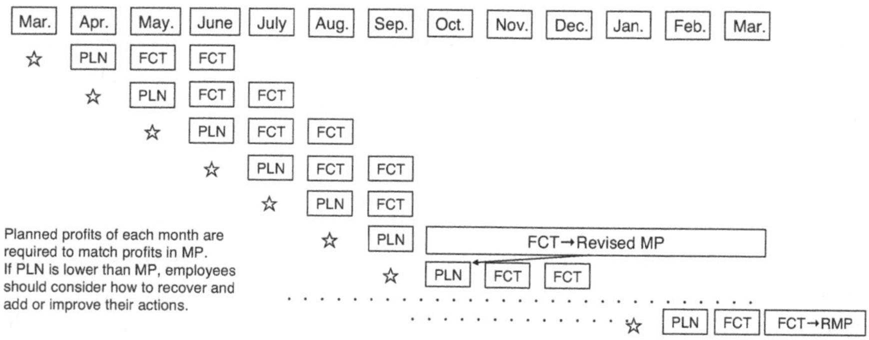

Figure 11.2 Rolling forecast in Kyocera

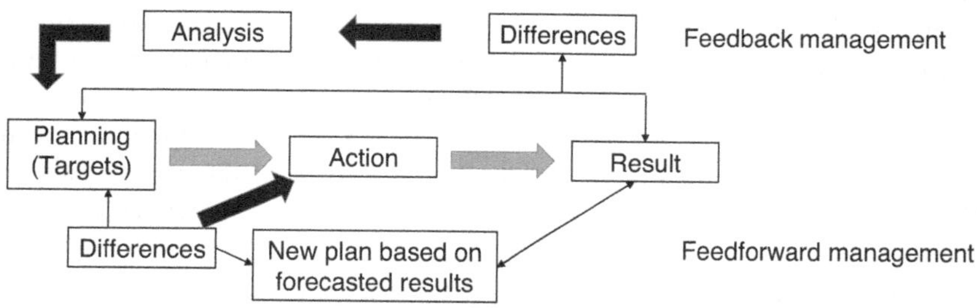

Figure 11.3 Feedforward and feedback management in Kyocera

feedforward management. Amoeba leaders compare the profit in MP with the forecasted one, and if there is a gap between them, new action plans to accomplish the profit target in MP are considered and implemented. Second, at the end of every month, Kyocera does feedback control by comparing actual profits with new planned profits, and new planned profits with target profits in MP. The important thing is to review the difference between forecasted and actual results, because in the case of Kyocera, new planned profits are not simply forecasted but become new targets.

As shown in Figure 11.3, Kyocera integrates a feedback system with a feedforward one into one management system. In other words, based on the comparison of MP and forecasted and newly planned amounts, as well as the comparison of MP and actual amounts used in the feedback system, the system to revise the plan is incorporated into the management system.

This is the extremely important point. A forecast is simply a forecast. As pointed out in BBM, the purpose for forecasting is to see changing environments and take new action to reach the target. The Kyocera management system has a process in which not only a forecast is made but also a new plan is made or the MP is modified to fill the gap immediately if a gap between forecasts and targets is seen. Without this process, it seems to be difficult to use a forecast effectively.

Transparency – open book management

Amoeba leaders have to attend the performance review meeting at the end of every month and give an explanation in detail about performance results of this month, changed plans for the next month, and forecasts for the following two months. Because a lot of amoebas conducting similar businesses like this exist in Kyocera, if an amoeba sets planned profits of the next month too low, it is exposed to other amoebas.

And even though an amoeba leader is able to set planned profits of the next month low by gaming, it will be revealed to other amoeba leaders that the planned profits are too low at the end of the next month.

In Kyocera it also is not accepted that actual profits not only fall below but also exceed planned profits modified monthly. That is because planned profits based on a forecast do not have stretch.

Thus, amoeba leaders have to always set the best targets because all the information is disclosed to their peers as well as their bosses. However, although amoebas' HE and income statements are disclosed, there is little relationship between their HE and income statement and amoeba members' bonuses. A bonus is decided by the profits of the whole company. Therefore, the reward system is a kind of holistic system.

5. Similarity between the Kyocera amoeba management and 12 principles of beyond budgeting

Leadership principles

Table 11.5 shows similarities between the Kyocera management system and leadership principles by Bogsness (2009) that I have stated previously.

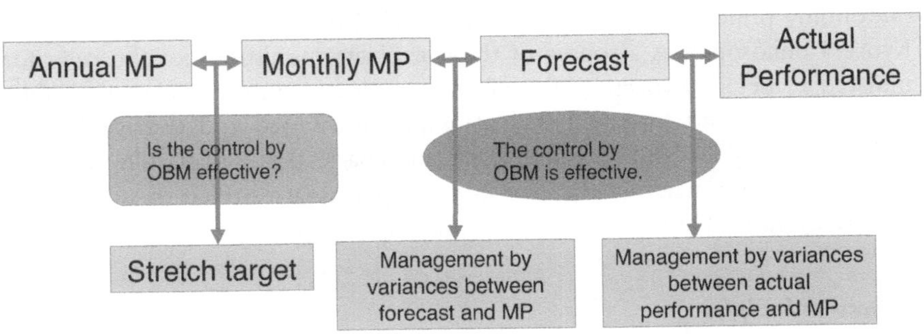

Figure 11.4 Open book management in Kyocera

Adapted from Kazusa, Y. The research of the construction in the amoeba management system and the total optimization, The Academic Study Group of the Amoeba Management ed. (2010) *Amoeba Management*, KCCS Management Consulting. (2010, p. 84).

Table 11.5 Comparing the Kyocera system with the beyond budgeting model (1)

Leadership principles	*Bogsnes (2009), p. 55*	*Kyocera system*
1 Customers	Focus everyone on improving customer outcomes, not on hierarchical relationships.	Kyocera focuses on the outside market, or customers.
2 Organization	Organize as a network of lean, accountable teams, not around centralized functions.	Each amoeba is lean and an accountable team.
3 Responsibility	Enable everyone to act and think like a leader, not merely follow the plan.	Each amoeba leader acts and thinks to make profits by their decision making.
4 Autonomy	Give teams the freedom and capability to act; do not micromanage them.	Each amoeba has the freedom and capability to act.
5 Values	Govern through a few clear values, goals, and boundaries, not detailed rules and budgets.	Every employee acts based on the Kyocera philosophy.
6 Transparency	Promote open information for self-management: do not restrict it hierarchically.	HE is opened to all the employees. Forecasted and actual IS is also opened at the performance review meeting.

First, it is customers rather than the internal workings of the organization that Kyocera focuses on (customers principle). Second, Kyocera is managed by a lot of small, divided units called amoebas, each of which has responsibility for HE and profits (organization principle). Third, amoeba leaders make decisions so that their amoebas can earn a profit, take actions on the decision, and have responsibility for the result of the actions (responsibility principle). For this reason, amoeba leaders are empowered to make decisions and take actions (autonomy principle). An amoeba is controlled based on the principles called Kyocera philosophy as a source of the organization culture, not the rules formulated in detail. Kyocera philosophy has a large number of contents (Value principle). HE and forecast-based plans are distributed and discussed at the various meetings. Thanks to this, other amoeba leaders and middle managers are able to know whether the plan has an appropriate stretch or not. That is how Kyocera is able to avoid gaming on setting a goal.

Process principles

Next, I will apply the Kyocera management system to the process principles, as shown in Table 11.6. It shows that the management tools used by Kyocera match the beyond budgeting principles.

Table 11.6 Comparing the Kyocera system with the beyond budgeting model (2)

Process principles	*Bogsnes (2009), p. 55*	*Kyocera system*
7 Goals	Set relative goals for continuous improvement; do not negotiate fixed performance contracts.	Each amoeba sets a target of HE and added value. HE is compared among amoebas. But Kyocera as a whole does not have relative targets.
8 Rewards	Reward shared success based on relative performance, not on meeting fixed targets.	HE and added value of each amoeba are scarcely linked with employees' bonus.
9 Planning	Make planning a continuous and inclusive process, not a top-down annual event.	Each amoeba uses a certain type of rolling forecast and rolling plan.
10 Controls	Base controls on relative indicators and trends, not on variances against plan.	Each amoeba is controlled by the HE and variances against MP and forecast, and actual performance and MP.
11 Resources	Make resources available as needed, not through annual budget allocations.	Each amoeba makes resources available as needed.
12 Coordination	Coordinate interactions dynamically, not through annual planning cycles.	Coordination with each amoeba is interactive.

HE of each amoeba is disclosed monthly to all the employees as a league table. Therefore, amoeba leaders make efforts to improve their HE and raise the rank in the league table. This is a counterpart of relative goals for continuous improvement of goals principles. However, profit targets of amoebas are basically fixed targets, and Kyocera as a whole does not have relative targets for the rank in the industry.

HE and profit targets are not directly connected to a bonus of each amoeba leader. The bonus depends on company-wide profit amounts, although of course an amoeba leader who achieves outstanding performance gets a promotion.

Kyocera makes a forecast for three months ahead and reviews the plan of the following month monthly in order to achieve MP. This just means flexibly remaking a plan on rolling forecasts and is a counterpart of the planning principle. Control by relative HE is a counterpart of the controls principle. By checking the difference between original MP and a new plan on forecasts and the difference between the plan and actual performance, control is exercised to reach annual targets. If resources which are not included in the original MP are needed, an amoeba leader is able to use the resources by consulting a manager (resources principle). Finally, coordination is exercised by a close interaction between production amoebas and sales amoebas, and each amoeba aims to realize MP.

6. Discussion

The Kyocera management model (KMM) is management without a budgeting system. However, differing from the case of Disco, I cannot say clearly that Kyocera has no budgeting systems. The MP is the financial plan of revenues and costs and its function is the same as the function of a budgeting system. Inamori understands the negative effects of a budget and devised KMM to overcome them. The amoeba system and Kyocera philosophy are two halves of the same whole. Even though BBM and KMM are developed in different countries and by different persons, this idea is also the same as BBM except for one point, for Kyocera clearly has the financial plan (master plan).

Comparing Kyocera and Disco, the management system in Disco is a type of pure BBM, and KMM is an improved model of BBM. I call it the KPI forecast management model. KMM is more readily accepted by many companies than the Disco management model. In fact, a consulting subsidiary of Kyocera has developed and sells KMM, and many companies have introduced it.

Inamori has aimed to keep achieving higher performance since the establishment of Kyocera in 1959. For this purpose, the entire staff has employed measures by trial and error to strive for higher performance. Consequently, the present management system was completed. He thought that all employees should continuously have a flexible plan by using a forecast in order to obtain a goal. In addition, he empowered front-line managers, or amoeba leaders, and

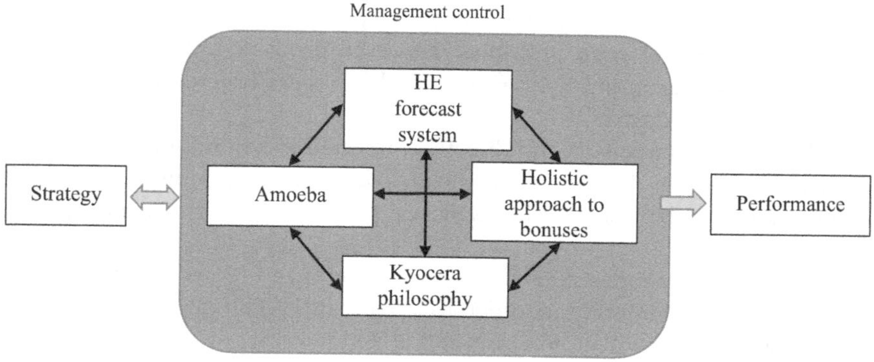

Figure 11.5 Strategic implementing system in Kyocera

inspired them to strive for maximization of amoebas' profits. He plainly explained knowledge about management accounting as HE and the internal income statement. Consequently, amoeba leaders understood that maximization of profits in each amoeba directly led to maximization of profits in the whole company. Amoeba leaders increase sales, reduce costs, and plan to use working hours effectively by themselves. Management tools to do these are counterparts of various process principles, as shown in Table 11.6.

However, KMM does not entirely consist of management tools. In order to carry out these management tools properly, that is, to set a stretch target, aim for the optimization of the company, eliminate various gamings, and form an organization able to cope with changes in the environment, Inamori created the Kyocera philosophy and taught all employees that they should do the right thing as human beings. Not all the management tools can work correctly without the strong values of the Kyocera philosophy.

The Kyocera management system was created in Far Eastern Japan, geographically and culturally so far from Northern Europe, or the home of beyond budgeting. Nevertheless it is surprising that these two systems are quite alike in content. This seems to reveal a clue to the universal solution to problems with budgets. Whether a company has a budget or not, and whether it uses BSC and ABC or not, it is able to conduct better management. The case of Kyocera shows that.

However, only some Japanese companies use KMM, and even the companies adopting amoeba management do not necessarily have the same form of use as the basic amoeba management. A company adopting amoeba management in the hospitality industry and Japan Airlines have the income statement of each organization but do not use HE for their management. The companies individually use an effective device for allocating indirect costs. The important thing is not to adopt a management tool but to build up the organization culture aiming to achieve a goal through the organization. The tool should be coordinated by the ideas of the individual company.

As mentioned before, Japanese companies do not have much dissatisfaction with the budgeting system. That seems to be because Japanese companies made different improvements to the budgeting system. The Kyocera management system is considered to be a case of those improved systems, and furnishes useful information to many companies that have big trouble with budgeting systems.

This chapter is adapted from Shimizu (2015).

References

Bogsnes, B. (2009) *Implementing Beyond Budgeting: Unlocking the Performance Potential*, Hoboken, NJ: John Wiley & Sons.

Cooper, R. (1995) *When Lean Enterprises Collide: Competing through Confrontation*, Boston, MA: Harvard Business School Press.

Cooper, R. and R.S. Kaplan (1998) *Cost and Effect*, Boston, MA: Harvard Business School Press.

Hope, J. and R. Fraser (2003a) Who needs budgets? *Harvard Business Review*, 81(2), 118–115.

Hope, J. and R. Fraser (2003b) *Beyond Budgeting: How Managers Can Break Free from the Annual Performance Trap*, Boston, MA: Harvard Business School Press.

Kazusa, Y. (2010) The research of the construction in the amoeba management system and the total optimization, in The Academic Study Group of the Amoeba Management (ed.) *Amoeba Management*, Chapter 2, Tokyo, Japan: KCCS Management Consulting, pp. 58–88. Written in Japanese.

Miya, H. (2003) *The Theory of AMOEBA Management*, Toyo Keizai Inc. Written in Japanese.

Shimizu, T. (2015) A comparison of the KPI forecast management model of Japanese companies and the Beyond Budgeting Model, *Waseda Business Review*, 443, 1–21.

12 The story of a comeback from bankruptcy

Japan Airlines

Key learning points

- Many full-service air carriers became bankrupt, including Japan Airlines (JAL), a Japanese national flag carrier. Why did it go bankrupt?
- JAL relisted only 32 months after its bankruptcy, and its financial performance has been much better than before bankruptcy.
- The Kyocera management model (KMM) was introduced at JAL. However, it is a little bit different from KMM in the manufacturing industry. What are the differences?

1. Introduction

Many full-service air careers (FSCs) face tough issues: a tight race among internal and foreign competitors, the rise of low-cost carriers (LCCs), and many event risks such as terrorism and pandemics. More than a few FSCs run into financial trouble. Alitalia-Societa Aerea Italiana is affiliated with Etihad Airways. Malaysia Airlines is nationalized. Almost all FSCs filed Chapter Eleven in the United States.[1]

In Japan, Japan Airlines (JAL) went bankrupt in 2010. It started as a parastatal company and was operated as a national flag carrier for almost 50 years. However, surprisingly JAL was relisted in 2012, only 32 months after its bankruptcy. Now, although its net sales are lower than those of All Nippon Airways, JAL is a highly profitable company. Why did JAL make a comeback from bankruptcy so early? In 2010, the selection of a rebuilder of JAL got in a tangle because it seemed so difficult to rebuild JAL, which was in bad financial condition and lost its reputation as an air carrier. Inamori, the founder of Kyocera, was named as the rebuilder, and finally he assented to it.

He introduced Kyocera management model (KMM) into JAL. How did he and his team succeed in changing the corporate culture of JAL from bureaucratic and rigid to self-governing and flexible? This chapter tells the story of a company that struggled with its own culture and accomplished organization innovation with the assistance of a new management control system.

2. The company outline

The history of Japan Airlines

JAL started in 1951, and it was the first airline after World War II. Based on the law, the Japanese government invested in JAL and owned half of its shares. In the beginning, JAL had only domestic lines but it started to operate international flights, Tokyo–San Francisco and Tokyo–Honolulu, in 1954. JAL encountered competition with U.S. carriers. However, it introduced large airplanes (DC-8) into international routes in 1960 and experienced a rise in performance with an increase in foreign tourists visiting Japan because of the Tokyo Olympics Games and an increase in Japanese tourists to go abroad because of the cancellation of the restrictions on overseas travel in the 1960s. In the 1970s, JAL had some accidents, including two jet crashes in New Delhi and Moscow. Moreover, an airplane of JAL was hijacked by Japanese extremists, the Japanese Red Army, in 1977. Also, in the 1970s, the financial performance of JAL was falling due to an oil shock and a downturn in the economy following it. Because a circular notice stipulated that JAL was assigned to operations of domestic mainlines and international lines in 1972, JAL abandoned its local lines.[2]

The management condition of JAL in the 1980s was generally good with the so-called bubble economy. By repeal of the circular notice shown previously, JAL entered into profitable local lines. However, it meant growing competition with ANA and TDA for international lines and domestic mainlines. JAL was privatized in 1987 and went on with the diversification strategy. Then, the financial performance of JAL in the 1990s seesawed. It nosedived due to excess investment in the hotel industry, a decrease in travelers due to the Gulf War, bursting of the bubble economy, and other factors. JAL got through the difficult situation by selling off some hotels and downsizing unprofitable lines.

Finally, simultaneous slowdown of the world economy caused by the terrorism event of September 11 and SARS, and Lehman Brothers bankruptcy dealt the final blow to JAL. It filed for bankruptcy – a reorganization plan in January 2010.

Although the selection of a rebuilder proved a challenge, Inamori was named new CEO. He accepted it and started to reform JAL, in which a bureaucratic mood was rampant as a result of being a long-term parastatal.

JAL requested debt write-offs, downsized its airline routes, allocated new shares to a third party, and dismissed many employees. At the same time, Inamori introduced KMM into JAL. He was committed to making critical changes, including satisfying customers, building employee trust and cooperation, and maximizing profits. After many fights with employees, Inamori put great faith in them and relisted JAL on the Tokyo Stock Exchange in September 2012.

Financial performance

As stated previously, the financial performance of JAL repeatedly seesawed. Table 12.1 shows the financial performance from right before bankruptcy to fiscal year 2015.

There are two features in financial results of JAL before and after bankruptcy. First, net sales decreased around 40 percent before bankruptcy, although they gradually increased from 2011. Second, profitability extremely improved. Both of these features resulted from the management reform (see Table 12.1).

JAL had a lot of too-large airplanes such as the Boeing 747 and many unprofitable domestic lines. Mass transportation in which air carriers carry many people at once with a large airplane is effective. Using the B-747 is profitable only when the plane is almost fully booked. However, many events that occurred in the 21st century had an enormous impact on JAL. The B-747 often transported just "air." Under this situation, an air carrier must allocate an appropriate size airplane. JAL introduced the B-777, which was more fuel-efficient than the B-747. Before then, the B-747 was the only large airplane for long distance routes. JAL had many B-747s and could not change them to small airplanes. The bureaucratic organization caused this problem. Once JAL set a plan of an airplane, it never changed it.

In addition, JAL had many types of airplanes.[3] When JAL merged with JAS, it took over almost all of JAS's airplanes and domestic routes. The more different types of airplanes an air carrier has, the higher costs it incurs because of many mechanics and parts for each type of airplane required to maintain airplanes. JAL also had many domestic routes, which raised costs because ground crews for airplane maintenance and ground workers were required.

JAL narrowed its seven aircraft types to four and closed unprofitable international and domestic routes, which contributed toward cutting costs and making profits. However, this is only one aspect of the story about the revival of JAL.

Table 12.1 Financial performance (billion yen)

	Net sales	*Operating income*	*Net income after tax*
2008	2,230.4	90.0	16.9
2009	1,951.2	–50.9	–63.2
2011	1,204.8	204.9	186.6
2012	1,238.8	195.2	171.7
2013	1,309.3	166.8	166.3
2014	1,344.7	179.7	153.9
2015	1,336.6	209.1	181.0

Adapted from financial reports of Japan Airlines

3. The process of revival

Why did JAL go bankrupt?

In addition to the structural reasons for bankruptcy as discussed previously, there also were psychological reasons. These include:

- Nobody in JAL expected that the national flag carrier would go bankrupt.
- Nobody was cost (and profit) conscious.
- There was no interaction between divisions.
- The mind-set was focused on "manuals," not on customers (Indo, 2013, pp. 39–48).

All employees knew the critical conditions of JAL but they believed that the Japanese government could help JAL by asking banks to finance JAL because it was once a parastatal organization.

Before bankruptcy, the financial information of profitability about each route was disclosed three months later. Therefore, managers only knew profits or losses of a route for the past three months – for example the North America route, the Europe route, and the Asian route. No manager was motivated to make profits in this situation.

JAL's organization was bureaucratic and sectionalism was rampant in it. Each division did not interfere in other divisions' management and did not want to be interfered with. All employees worked according to the manual of their divisions and did not interact with other divisions and departments to improve their operations. Additionally, managers had little tendency to absorb a business plan made by a corporate development department. Worse yet, labor unions were so powerful that management could not help but accept many claims.

Two main initiatives to reconstruct JAL

Inamori embarked upon the reconstruction of JAL and introduced two categories of initiatives: "education for leadership" and "the introduction of a self-supporting system."

The first profound message from Inamori was "to be a leader, not a manager." We may feel that leaders and managers are the same, but the meaning is a little different. According to the Oxford Dictionary, a leader is "a person who leads or commands a group, organization, or country," and a manager is "a person responsible for controlling or administering an organization or group of staff." Leaders lead many people to do the best work for companies, not just to control performance.

In the book *Implementing Beyond Budgeting* (Bogsnes, 2009, pp. 192–195), the author makes an interesting comment. Leaders must focus on the performance problem, such as trust, cost, targets, and evaluation. On the other hand, managers put emphasis on the efficiency problem. This is the same idea as Inamori's. As indicated in the previous chapter, there are so many similar points between Inamori's management philosophy and leadership principles, and the amoeba system and process principles.

Leaders must show the way to a goal and go ahead of others. Inamori placed top priority on a program of education for leadership. JAL also made a corporate policy and a "JAL philosophy" that clearly shows the mental set to realize its corporate policy.

The second initiative is the introduction of a self-supporting system. Even though JAL has a perfect philosophy, it cannot manage its operation without appropriate and timely management information. The important thing is that all employees timely understand their performance and consider what they should do to improve their performance. JAL introduced KMM developed by Inamori. It is a type of amoeba system that includes a forecasting system, internal income statement to support managers' decision making, and relative targets, but there are some differences from the amoeba system in Kyocera.

How did JAL introduce the new management system? In the next section, I will explain this.

4. JAL corporate policy and JAL philosophy

The JAL corporate policy is as follows:

The JAL group will:

> Pursue the material and intellectual growth of all our employees;
> Deliver unparalleled service to our customers;
> and
> Increase corporate value and contribute to the betterment of society.
> (http://www.jal.com/en/outline/corporate/philosophy.html)

Before bankruptcy, JAL did not seem to focus on customers. Needless to say, customer satisfaction is critical for companies to earn sales. The new JAL corporate policy clearly states this point. This corporate policy also emphasizes the happiness of all employees, like the Kyocera corporate policy.

The JAL philosophy is a code of conduct to attain the corporate policy.

> JAL Philosophy
> Part 1 In order to lead a wonderful life
>
> > Chapter 1 The formula for success
> > Chapter 2 Have the right attitude
> > Chapter 3 Accumulate tedious efforts with passion
> > Chapter 4 Ability to improve

Part 2 To become a wonderful JAL

Chapter 1 Each of us makes what JAL it is
Chapter 2 Have a keen sense of profitability
Chapter 3 Unite our hearts
Chapter 4 Possess a fighting spirit
Chapter 5 Be creative in our work
(http://www.jal.com/en/outline/corporate/conduct.html)

The entire philosophy indicates a mind-set to do the right things for employees themselves and for JAL. Chapter 1 is interesting. In this chapter, the formula for success is as follows:

The Result of Life and Work = Attitude[4] × Effort × Ability

Here, effort and ability range widely, but they are positive values. In contrast, attitude may take on negative values. Even though people have excellent ability and do their work with every effort, bad attitudes produce negative results. JAL has had many excellent and skilled employees since before bankruptcy. Inamori thought their bureaucratic attitudes had caused problems, and felt a need to change their mind-sets. He adopted some norms to encourage employees to think positively, with the company's best interest in mind.

In part 2, the JAL philosophy mentions that employees should contribute to the success of JAL. Some examples are: "put yourself in the customer's position, maximize revenues and minimize expenses, elevate our cost-consciousness, and manage the company based on accurate figures."

In fact, all of these are "common sense" for everybody, not only in JAL but also in other companies. However, it is so difficult to do what is expected. One of the strengths of Toyota lies in this attitude. All managers and employees make every effort to increase profits, to increase sales, and to decrease costs every day. The just-in-time system is a famous production system, and Toyota discloses this system to other companies. However, not so many companies succeed in introducing this system because this system is based on employees' dedicated efforts to cut costs as well as to boost quality.

JAL had introduction meetings for all people in JAL to have them understand the essence of the JAL philosophy. Understandably, many people felt strange about the JAL philosophy because it was not so special and everybody knew it as common sense.

JAL started the education of the JAL philosophy to have all employees understand it deeply. First, a facilitator delivered a lecture on the JAL philosophy. Next, employees talked about their experiences and tasks on site and discussed their idea based on the philosophy. They shared their thoughts and ideas on the philosophy and also considered what they lacked and what they should do to recover JAL.

5. Self-supporting system

JAL prepared the JAL philosophy as a code of conduct and introduced the Kyocera management system as a self-supporting system. This system uses a division income statement. Each division calculates its gain and loss. Before bankruptcy, JAL reported gain and loss of each route three months later. However, most pilots and cabin attendants were not interested in this information because it was not delivered to them in a timely manner. They only needed to perform their duties.

Change of the organization

One of the reasons for a lack of cost-consciousness lies in JAL's organization structure before bankruptcy. At that time, the corporate planning division made all management accounting data. For example, central office costs were allocated by the decision of this division, and operating divisions did not give serious consideration to those allocated costs and concentrated on the operation without cost-consciousness. To get rid of this problem, calculate and open financial information of each operating division, and assist each division to consider its profitability, first JAL changed its organization as shown in Figure 12.1.

Managing Division Passenger Sales (MDPS) sells air tickets directly to customers. *Managing Division Route Marketing* (MDRM) is responsible for operations of domestic and international routes. This division manages all operations of flights and buys all services from four supporting divisions. This division must decide the best combination of equipment and all services from support divisions. The cargo and mail division sells freight transportation services and postal services to customers and commissions MDRM to deliver them. Four supporting divisions deliver their services, pilots, CAs, engineering and maintenance services, and ground operation services to MDRM.

Thus, MDPS, MDRM, and the cargo and mail division are real profit centers. Although flight operations, engineering and maintenance, cabin attendants, and airport operations divisions are cost centers in essence, JAL sets them as profit centers by using transfer pricing.

Transfer pricing

Each supporting division that delivers its services to MDRM must book sales. JAL sets the transfer price for every transaction among MDRM, MDPS, and the cargo and mail division, as well as between MDRM and supporting divisions. For example, when MDRM commissions the engineering and maintenance division to check an airplane before flight, it pays a predetermined transfer price. The transfer price is set for each transaction between MDRM and other support divisions. Each division does not have authority to set or negotiate transfer prices. The corporate planning department sets all transfer prices for internal transactions to give a small profit to each division. When divisions control their

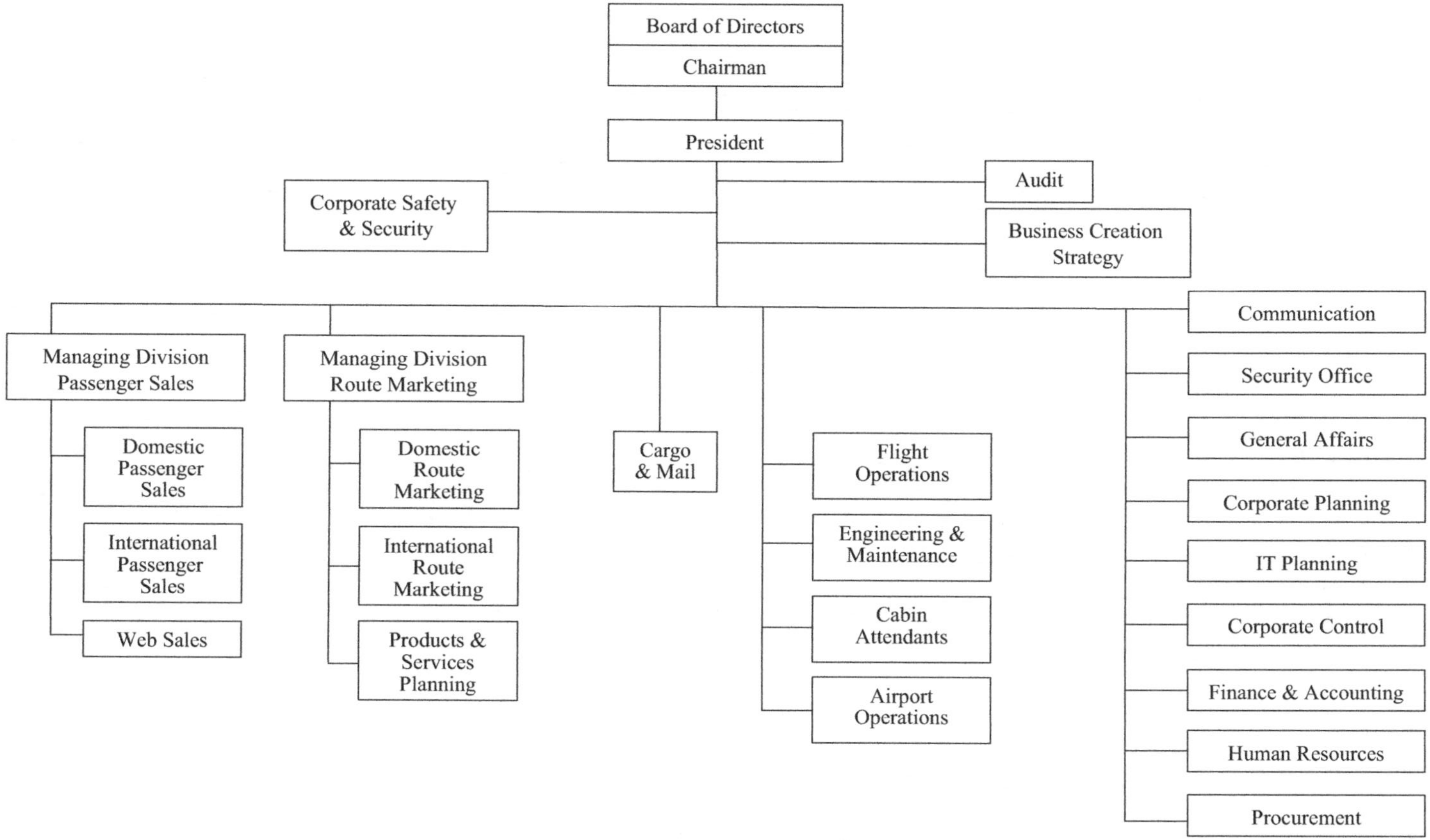

Figure 12.1 JAL organization chart in April 2016 (as of September 2016)
Adapted from http://www.jal.com/en/outline/corporate/organization.html

costs at predetermined (budgeted) levels, they make profits. These transfer prices are reviewed every half year according to changes in the market.

Business flow in JAL

Customers pay airfare to MDPS. It has sales forces and makes an effort to sell as much as possible. MDPS transfers all sales amounts to MDRM and receives sales commissions from MDRM. This system is the same as the amoeba system in Kyocera. Sales commissions are MDPS's revenues, and MDPS calculates its profits by deducting its costs from revenues. Although the rate of sales commissions is decided by the central office, MDPS can earn profits by its own efforts.

MDRM has some departments and divisions, such as Domestic Route Marketing, International Route Marketing, and Route Planning. Domestic Route Marketing and International Route Marketing play a key role in this business model. I will now take domestic routes as an example.

Domestic Route Marketing (DRM) is responsible for all operations of a flight. Assume that it plans a flight from Haneda (Tokyo) to Fukuoka. DRM hires an airplane from an airplane division (by way of the route planning department). To operate this airplane, DRM hires pilots and cabin attendants from the flight operation division and cabin attendants division. DRM also asks the Maintenance and Engineering division for ship maintenance and Airport Operation division for ground operations. It pays some money (transfer prices) in exchange for these services.

The Cargo and Mail division has its own customers. It receives orders from customers and requests delivery of DRM.

As just described, each division has its revenues and controls costs to make profits. For example, DRM coordinates all functions to operate one flight. If the predicted number of passengers is relatively small, that is to say, the equipment is too large, DRM may change the equipment (e.g., B-767 to B-737) to reduce operation costs. This type of decision never occurred before bankruptcy because changing equipment needed a lot of preparation work. Now, DRM makes a rough estimate of profits or losses of one flight and attempts to earn profits to operate it.

Supporting divisions also have internal income statements. Thus, employees of these divisions have come to consider a way of making profits mainly by cutting costs. It is so important to confirm the JAL philosophy teaches a sense of profitability and the right direction for human action.

The following is a famous story about a maintenance shop. Engineers used gloves only once and then threw them away, even though they were reusable. Now gloves are washed and used time after time. In this shop, parts of aircrafts were housed in one type of plastic bag, regardless of the size of a part. In many cases, the bag of a fixed size was too big for a part, and of course, it was more costly than a bag of the right size. Now there are bags of different sizes and engineers use the appropriately sized bags. The accumulation of these small savings resulted in a big cost reduction and an increase in profits.

The previous example may be taken as a matter of course. When we buy something expensive, for example a car, we often check specifications and compare some types to negotiate with a car dealer about the price. When we need to get some gas, we go to a cheaper gas station. People must also do in the company what they do in their lives. However, employees in companies tend to neglect to make such an effort. Thus, companies need a code of conduct such as the JAL philosophy that leads employees to do the right thing.

In addition to cost reduction, it is necessary to put forth a great effort to increase revenues. For example, cabin attendants can sell more goods in in-flight sales. They are sometimes involved in the selection of goods from the perspective of customers. The most important thing to increase revenues is "to get customer satisfaction." Price competition is heating up because of the rise of LCCs. JAL does not want to be involved in this situation, and employs a differentiation strategy so that customers select JAL even though airfares of JAL are more expensive than those of other air carriers, because of good services and comfort and the convenient flight experience.

I have heard an interesting story relating to passenger comfort. A cabin attendant found that some passengers in economy class felt cramped in small seats. All passengers in economy class (including me) know that seats are uncomfortable, but they undergo such hardships in exchange for low airfares. This is common sense in the airline industry. JAL started JAL philosophy education sessions at that time. Chapter 1 in part 2 of the JAL philosophy says "Each of us makes JAL what it is." It teaches every employee how to be the person who makes JAL an excellent air carrier. An additional part of the philosophy says, "Put yourself in the customer's position." The new JAL values customers' satisfaction and has all employees walk in the customers' shoes. As a result, a cabin attendant consulted with her superior, and the CAs division made a proposal to introduce larger seats. Central officers felt confused about it. Although wider seats would get customer satisfaction, JAL needed to invest in new seats and decrease the number of seats. Finally, JAL made a decision to develop a new seat in economy class to give customers a more comfortable experience. JAL improved the form of seats and succeeded to widen legroom by 5 cm.

6. Discussions

Figure 12.2 shows management control in JAL. Its organizational structure is a functional system. JAL has some functional divisions and treats them as profit centers. All divisions have internal income statements and calculate their own profits. They can manage every operation to make profits and put many ideas about cost reductions and higher profits into action. JAL holds many meetings to review actual performance and the plan of the next month, just the same as Kyocera. In these meetings, all information that division leaders have is disclosed. This information includes reasons behind actual performance and the next month plan. Because all divisions cooperate to provide customers with a good flight, even if a division leader tries to set a lower target, top management (and other leaders) see through his or her intention. Social control works here. The JAL

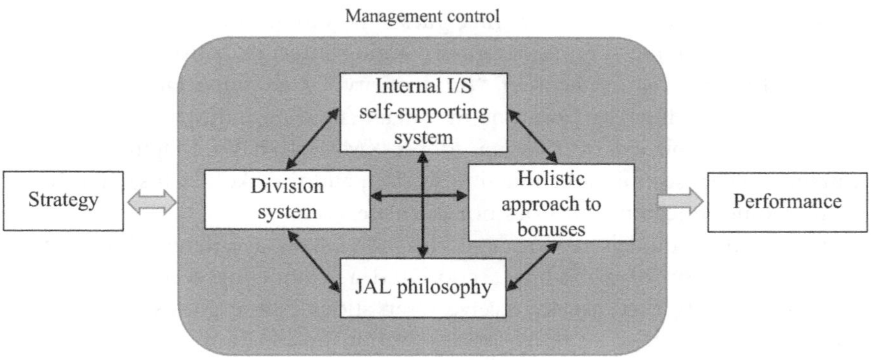

Figure 12.2 Strategic implementing system in JAL

philosophy plays an important role in having employees do the right things both for JAL and for themselves. It plays the same role as the Kyocera philosophy.

JAL uses KMM as a management accounting tool. However, there are some differences between Kyocera and JAL.

First, although amoebas in Kyocera are real microprofit centers, some divisions in JAL are pseudo-profit centers. This point relates to the second point, the difference of the business process structure. In Kyocera, manufacturing amoebas and sales amoebas are continuous processes,[5] and one manufacturing amoeba is also a part of a continuous manufacturing process. In many cases, there are market prices of transferred products. Even if there is no market price, all amoebas know the price of the final product, and all amoeba leaders negotiate their transfer prices to share profits with all participants.

In contrast, the business process of JAL is not continuous. MDRM organizes all flights by procuring staff, an airplane, and many services to operate one flight. There are many cases in which MDRM cannot find rational market prices and cannot set transfer prices for all transactions by negotiating them with other divisions. Therefore, transfer prices are decided by the corporate planning division by trial and error. However, all decisions of Will Rewards and Painful Charges in Disco are made by parties to a transaction. Thus, these transfer prices may be decided the same as Kyocera and Disco in the future.

In addition, each division in JAL has its own income statement, but it does not calculate hourly efficiency (HE). In the amoeba system, measuring working time and waiting or idle time is required to calculate HE in the internal income statement. This is easy for manufacturing companies because they measure and report their working time for each product that they make and waiting time in their work reports. However, dividing total working hours into two parts (working time and waiting time) is not easy for a service industry. Consider reception desk clerks of a city hotel for example. Their jobs are check-in operations, check-out operations, and answering guests' inquiries. However, clerks also do other jobs, including waiting for guests during intervals between these operations. Although the concept of "productivity" is so important in a service industry, this is different from one in a manufacturing industry.

A city hotel owned by Kyocera adopts KMM. It has a lodging section, a restaurant/bars section, a banqueting section, and the like. Each section has its own income statement but does not calculate HE.

Management models of JAL and this hotel have a different feature from KMM. It is easy for a lodging section and a banqueting section to forecast revenues because they usually receive reservations before guests visit a hotel.[6] Thus, leaders of these sections use reservation information as the forecast to attain their master plan.

As mentioned previously, KMM is not a rigid management model but flexible depending on the circumstances surrounding companies and the features of an industry. The most important part about having a good management control system is that every company must have a good code of conduct. Even though a company has a good management control system such as BSC, BBM, or KMM, it is not enough to achieve good results. Top management should prepare a good code of conduct that reaches employees, and repeatedly emphasizes its importance with conviction.

Notes

1 Southwest Airlines is the only air carrier that has not experienced bankruptcy in the United States. It is usually classified as a low-cost carrier (LCC).
2 ANA was assigned for domestic mainlines and local lines, and Toa Domestic Airlines (TDA) was assigned for local lines. TDA changed its designation to Japan Air System (JAS) and merged with JAL in 2006.
3 Before bankruptcy, JAL had seven types of airplanes. Now it has only four types: B-737, B-767, B-777, and B-787.
4 Attitude means a way of thinking.
5 According to Otani (2016), amoeba organizations are classified into two categories: a continuous amoeba and a discontinuous (a prime contractor type) amoeba. The amoeba system in Kyocera is a continuous and that in JAL is a discontinuous type.
6 According to our research (conducted with professor Otani at Nagasaki University) concerning Hotel Nikko Princess Kyoto, in the master plan, the forecast of revenues of each day in a month means the number of booked or reserved guests plus something extra.

References

Bogsnes, B. (2009) *Implementing Beyond Budgeting: Unlocking the Performance Potential*, Hoboken, NJ: John Wiley & Sons.

Indo, M. ed. (2013) *Regeneration of JAL*, Tokyo, Japan: Nikkei Publishing Inc. Written in Japanese.

Otani, H. (2016) *Service Reengineering and Amoeba Management*, the handout of the first Forum of the Japanese Association of Management Accounting.

Index

ABB 95–6
ABC 20, 22–5, 29, 65, 95
ABM 95
accounting frauds 6
action control 7, 14
activities 22; batch level 24
activity-based budgeting 95
activity-based costing 20
activity-based management 95
activity costs 23
allocation base 65
allocation bases of operating department costs 33
amoebas 138

Balanced Scorecard 13, 68–9
Bank of Tokyo-Mitsubishi 74
Bank of Tokyo-Mitsubishi UFJ 79n5
BBM 35, 119–20, 134–5, 146
beyond budgeting 119; concept of 120
beyond budgeting model 35, 119
book value per share 83
BPS 83
brand managers 100
BSC 68–9
budget 12
budgetary management 12
budgeting 94
budgeting system 35, 37, 51–2, 119; problem with 37, trouble with 120
business structure 81

capital asset pricing model 83
capital charge 83
capital turnover 81
CAPM 83
CAS 27–32
central office 57, 59
company system 59–60
company union system 74
confrontation strategy 71
contribution margin 61
controllable fixed costs 61
controllable profits 61
corporate costs 61–2, 64; allocation of 64
corporate philosophy 7
Cost Accounting Standards in Japan 27
cost-based transfer prices 109
cost basis 109
cost center 57–8
cost drivers 23
cost hierarchies 24
cost of capital 63–4
cost of debt 83
cost of equity 83
cost plus profit basis 110
cross-shareholdings 87
CT 81, 82, 88
cultural control 7, 14–15; in Japanese companies 15
current profit 132n7
customer perspective 70

decentralization 54–6
department costing system 21
diagnostic control systems 16
direct departmental overhead costs 21
direct financing 80
direct method 27
Disco 35, 126
Disco Values 10
division profits 62
division system 58, 106; in Japan 59
dual pricing 111, 115
dual-rate method 32

earnings before income and tax 82
earnings per share 83
economic value added 61, 83
ECSI 93

empowerment 5, 55
Enron 6
EPS 83
European Customer Satisfaction Index 93
EVA® 61, 80, 83, 85

facility-sustaining activities 24
familistic management 74
feedback control 142
feedforward management 142
financial performance of Disco 126; of JAL 151; of Kao 96–7; of Kyocera 136; of ME 114
financial perspective 69
five main principles of Toyoda 4
forecast system in NEC 124; in Kyocera 141
formula for success 153
FSCs 149
Fuji Xerox 74
full cost basis 109
full-service air careers 149
functional system 57, 106

genba-ism 98
General Electric 59
grouping step-down method 21

HE 138–9, 144–5
high-context communication 100
holistic approach 6, 122, 129
hosaku 77–8
Hoshin-Kanri 69, 76, 78; definition of 10; flow of 76
hourly efficiency 138

Inamori, K. 136, 149, 152–4
income statement by brand 100
income statements of decentralized organizations 61
indirect departmental overhead costs 21
indirect financing 80
in-house training 74
interactive control systems 16
internal capital 60
internal dividends 60
internal interest 61
internal process perspective 70
investment center 57, 116
investment turnover 63
Iwasaki. Y 112

JAL 149
JAL philosophy 153
Japan Airlines 149
Japan Quality Award 73

Kaizen 75
Kanebo 104n9
Kansai Electric Power 74
Kao 92, 96
Kao Way 98–9
keiei-rinen 76
keijo-rieki 85
keiretsu 87
Kirin Brewery 74
KMM 137–8, 146–7, 149, 153, 159
KPI forecast management model 130, 134
Kyocera 7, 35, 134, 136
Kyocera Management Model 137, 146, 149
Kyocera philosophy 137

labor costs per hour 140
LCCs 149
LCPH 140
leadership principles 124
league table 122, 138
learning and growth perspective 70
leverage 82, 88
lifetime employment 6, 74
low-context communication 99
low-cost carriers 149

main-bank system 87
management accounting 11
management control 12
management control systems 1; as a package 16
market-based price 108
market-based price minus some avoidable costs incurred by internal transactions 109
marketing costs 92–3
master plan 138
matrix income statement in ME 116–17
Matsushita, K. 5, 55, 136
MCSs 1; Japanese 5
measures 73
microprofit centers 135
mission 125
mission of Disco 127
Mitsubishi Electric 112
MP 138, 140, 145

Nagase, S. 96
NEC 124

negotiated pricing 110
net operating profit after tax 83
Nissan 75
NOPAT 83

open book management 143
operating departments 21, 27, 30
order filling costs 93
order getting costs 93
overhead costs 21

P&A 102
painful charge 130
Panasonic 4, 7, 55, 75
pay per performance system 6
performance innovation management 129
performance management accounting 11–12
performance measures of divisions 62
personnel control 6, 14
PIM 129
policy cost budgeting 94
PPP system 6, 13
process principles 121
production amoeba 138–9
production departments *see* operating departments
product-sustaining activities 24
profit & advertising 102
profit center 57–8, 116
pseudomicroprofit center 135

real microprofit center 135
reciprocal method 27
relative target 121, 139
relative target in Disco 128
residual income 62–3
responsibility center 57
result control 5, 14
return on assets 82
return on capital employed 82
return on equity 60, 80, 82
return on investment 62
return on sales 62, 81
revenue center 57–8
RI 62–3
Ricoh 74
risk-free rate of interest 84
risk premium 84
ROA 82
ROCE 82
ROE 60, 82–3, 85, 88, 121
ROI 62–4, 80–1, 85, 121
rolling forecast 123
ROS 62, 81–2, 88, 127

sales amoeba 138–9
scorecards 70–1
Sekiya, M. 126
self-supporting system 153, 155
selling, general and administrative expenses 92
seniority-based wages 6, 74
service departments *see* support departments
sha-kun 76
shared responsibilities 65
sha-ze 7
Statoil 130
step-down method 27
strategic formulation 12
strategic implementing system 15; in Disco 131; in JAL 159; in Kao 103, in Kyocera 146; in ME 117
strategic initiative 71, 73
strategic management systems 2
strategic objectives 70–1
strategy maps 69–70
support departments 21, 27, 29–30
Svenska Handelsbanken 119–22

target costing 46, 75
task control 12
Toshiba 6
Toyoda, S. 4
TOYODA KO-RYO *see* five main principles of Toyoda
Toyota 75
transfer price 13, 58, 106, 139, 155
transfer pricing 106, 155
transparency and trust 125

uncontrollable fixed costs 61
UNIQLO 70
unit-level activities 24

value propositions 70
variable cost basis 109
vertical supplier system 26

WACC 61, 83
weighted average capital cost 61, 83
will accounting 128
will reward 130

Yamazaki Baking Co., Ltd 56
yoki-monozukuri 98

zaibatsu 86
ZBB 94
zero-based budgeting 94
zero-based thinking 94